DESIGNED FC

If you're looking for ways to give back to your community, then this book, the first to profile thirteen projects designed and built by architects and Habitat for Humanity®, will help. Detailed plans, sections, and photographs show you how these projects came about, the strategies used by each team to approach the design and construction process, and the obstacles they overcame to realize a successful outcome. The lessons and insights, presented here will aid you, whether you're an architect, architecture student, Habitat affiliate leader, or an affordable housing advocate.

Located all across the United States, these projects represent the full spectrum of Habitat for Humanity affiliates, from large urban affiliates to small rural programs. These cases illustrate a broad range of innovative approaches to energy performance, alternative construction strategies, and responses to site context. And each house demonstrates that design quality need not fall victim to the rigorous imperatives of cost, delivery, and financing.

David Hinson is the head of the School of Architecture at Auburn University.

Justin Miller is an assistant professor at Auburn University's School of Architecture.

DESIGNED

FOR

HABITAT

Collaborations with Habitat for Humanity®

David Hinson and Justin Miller

Routledge
Taylor & Francis Group

NEW YORK AND LONDON

First published 2013
by Routledge
711 Third Avenue, New York, NY 10017

Simultaneously published in the UK
by Routledge
2 Park Square, Milton Park, Abingdon, Oxon OX14 4RN

Routledge is an imprint of the Taylor & Francis Group, an informa business

Library of Congress Cataloging in Publication Data
Hinson, David (David W.)
Designed for Habitat : collaborations with Habitat for Humanity / David Hinson
and Justin Miller.
    p. cm.
Includes bibliographical references and index.
1. Architects and community—United States. 2. Habitat for Humanity
International, Inc. I. Miller, Justin. II. Title. III. Title: Collaborations with Habitat
for Humanity.
  NA2543.S6H56 2012
  728–dc23
  2011039876

ISBN: 978-0-415-89108-0 (hbk)
ISBN: 978-0-415-89109-7 (pbk)
ISBN: 978-0-203-12347-8 (ebk)

Acquisition editor: Wendy Fuller
Project manager: Laura Williamson
Production editor: Alfred Symons
Text and cover designer: Jan Haux
Typesetter: Alex Lazarou

Printed and bound in India by Replika Press Pvt. Ltd.

DEDICATION

To our students, our Habitat partners, our families,
and to the families touched by these amazing projects.

CONTENTS

GROUP ONE
COLLABORATIONS WITH ARCHITECTURE SCHOOLS

GROUP TWO
COLLABORATIONS WITH ARCHITECTS

FOREWORD

Robert Ivey

Executive vice president/chief executive officer of the American Institute of Architects. From 1996 to 2010 he was vice president of McGraw-Hill Construction and editor in chief of *Architectural Record*. He is a native of Columbus, Mississippi, and currently resides in Washington, DC.

The name Habitat for Humanity® has gained international recognition, yet only relatively recently with the significant participation of the nation's architects. Today, however, architects are making a difference for the program, as this important book records and analyzes. *Designed for Habitat* also illuminates a trend in our profession. Many members in the current generation of architects want to design housing for low-income residents and are disposed to invest their time and talents in learning how to do it best.

A couple of markers in this trend can be found in New Orleans where, in the aftermath of Hurricane Katrina, architects joined efforts to build low-cost housing. On a completely cleared site in the flood-ravaged Lower Ninth Ward, the Brad Pitt-backed Make It Right Foundation and other non-profits are sponsoring construction of twenty-one houses. Talented architects from around the world, many with high name recognition, have based their designs on New Orleans house typologies and are producing striking individual results.

Meanwhile, across the Industrial Canal, Habitat for Humanity, with the involvement of New Orleans native musicians Branford Marsalis and Harry Connick Jr., and a workforce numbering an astonishing 70,000 volunteers, built Musicians Rainbow Village Row—seventy-two frame houses of identical design painted rainbow colors, plus ten elder-friendly apartments. Habitat's Rainbow Village is marked by simple construction of straightforward houses with front porches where musicians can sit outside and play. The project is coherent, harmonious, built, and occupied.

The distinctions between these two efforts are evident. One is turning out individual houses that are singular in design, while the Habitat project, less dependent on innovation, has clicked into place. But viewed together they reinforce the point that there is room for creative architecture and responsiveness to local culture when designing and building low-income houses.

It isn't hyperbole to say that one historic city's epic tragedy followed by a deep and long-lasting national economic recession redirected the priorities of many Americans, including designers. In the rarified world of international architecture, the biomorphic cultural icons, the acrophobic skyscrapers, the exuberant private Xanadus—design marvels that defined an era—began to seem more than a little beside the point. Leading the way, future architects lodged in design studios across the country had already reacted to indulgence.

Many were outside the traditional centers of fashion. Located in southeast Alabama, the School of Architecture, Planning, and Landscape Architecture at Auburn University has earned a reputation of excellence. In 2011, for instance, the architecture program was ranked the most admired in a poll of deans of architecture schools across the country. The Rural Studio, established in 1993, is a big part of that recognition. Each year architecture undergraduates build houses or community buildings in Black Belt communities in southwest Alabama. And so it should come as no surprise that Auburn is where the authors of this book reside and teach: David Hinson heads the school and Justin Miller is an assistant professor of architecture.

Habitat for Humanity International

As an architectural writer and editor (and a native Southerner) I've observed with interest and chronicled some of the accomplishments of Auburn students, as well as Habitat for Humanity International, the Americus, Georgia-based non-profit trailblazer in low-cost housing. Habitat was conceived at Koinonia Farm, a small, interracial Christian community near Americus, where in 1968 Millard Fuller and his wife Linda, along with volunteers and prospective homeowners, constructed a community of forty-two simple, concrete-block houses centered around four recreational acres. Fuller had made a small fortune in real estate in Montgomery, Alabama, and he and Linda became intent upon building "simple, decent houses" for low-income people. In 1973 they took the Koinonia model to Zaire and three years later founded Habitat. To date, Habitat has built more than 400,000 houses, according to its website, that shelter an estimated two million people worldwide.

Fuller, whom I had the opportunity to interview for an article and met on several other occasions (he died in 2009), had specific ideas about Habitat houses, that they should be simple enough and straightforward enough for volunteers to hammer together. At the time of one memorable Habitat experience for me twenty-one years ago—observing fourteen basic houses under construction during three brutally hot days in Miami—he seemed convinced that architectural nicety could, and probably would, usurp utilitarian necessity. By then, in 1990, the Habitat building process had become so well honed that the frames on the Miami houses went up in a day and a half and the synthetic stucco exterior walls were all in place by the end of the third day. I observed Jimmy and Rosalynn Carter, toiling in the heat on successive days alongside volunteer workers who, by Fuller's plan, included future occupants of those houses. All were enthusiastic members of a smoothly running construction crew.

Fuller's overriding preoccupation with simple construction, plus his wariness of architects, limited their involvement in Habitat's early years. Later, however, architects were brought into the organization and given an active role to play.

The Make It Right houses in New Orleans may imply to some people that architects are more interested in designing showplaces than in becoming engaged in the design of replicable and affordable prototype designs. This book suggests otherwise. It demonstrates to the lay leaders of Habitat for Humanity affiliates and other non-profits that capable and creative architects want to participate in the collaborative processes of solving problems in affordable housing.

Designed for Habitat

David Hinson's preface, "Seeking Common Ground," is an informed, concise, and plainspoken summary of our profession's sometimes misguided efforts in low-cost housing, but it's a well-grounded view of the future as well. And I especially commend David's and Justin Miller's final chapter, "Lessons from the Field: Keys to Making Collaborations Work." A central thesis there is that architects would best approach the Habitat process with an open mind.

There is much to learn. The hard truth, as David explains in the preface, is that today's architects have "very little current experience" designing for this market. In the field, architects are asked to work through their differences with clients, overcome such ingrained professional biases as devaluing standard design templates, and avoid common pitfalls when teaching students on the job. The rewards are manifestly abundant, including the pride in humanitarian accomplishment that the architects of the projects profiled on these pages can take. All thirteen excel as individual examples and collectively portend a bright future—for architects, for innovative Habitat projects, and for America's low-income residents.

PREFACE

Seeking Common Ground

David Hinson

In the summer of 2001, as I was planning my first design–build collaboration with Habitat for Humanity®, I discussed the impending project with Samuel Mockbee, my Auburn colleague and founder of Auburn's acclaimed Rural Studio.[1] Mockbee listened carefully to my plans and offered encouragement and advice, and a note of caution. He said, "Millard Fuller called me one day and tried to convince me that the Rural Studio should be designing homes for Habitat. I told him we would be happy to, provided he would commit to building a truly *decent* house."

Mockbee believed that homes designed for low-income families should do more than just provide shelter, that they should express the dignity and pride of these families and uplift their spirit, or as he described it, "provide shelter for the soul." Although he wished us well in our project he was skeptical that the values he believed in, values we shared, could ever find traction with a client such as Habitat for Humanity.

A few weeks later, during a field trip to the headquarters of Habitat for Humanity International (HFHI) in Americus, Georgia, Millard Fuller, Habitat's founder and visionary leader, seemed to confirm Mockbee's skepticism when he told me and my students that he equated the involvement of architects in Habitat projects with pressure to add unnecessary expense to home construction costs. "Every time you spend 10 percent more on a home, one out of ten families doesn't get a house," he told our group, adding, "This is Habitat for Humanity, not a Lottery for Humanity." Fuller seemed to equate "design" with extravagance, and he viewed any effort to bring up the issues we were concerned with as conflicting with Habitat's standard of "simple and decent" homes, and incompatible with Habitat's mission to "eradicate poverty housing."[2] Despite Fuller's inspiring passion for his organization and its mission, it was a sobering conversation for me and my students.

How could this gulf in perception about the role of design in affordable housing be bridged? Both Mockbee and Fuller made helping poor families a centerpiece of their life's work, yet their view for the role of design and designers in the process of creating affordable housing could not have been farther apart.

It was clear we would have to find more common ground than sharing a desire to help poor families in need of affordable housing. There would have to be a broader set of shared goals and understandings to make our partnership with Habitat succeed.

Architects and affordable-housing advocates have had a tumultuous relationship over the twentieth century. At times this partnership has been vital and fruitful, and at times misguided and destructive. There have been decades when architects have been at the forefront of the effort to respond to the affordable-housing challenge, and there have been decades when design was discredited and exiled from the toolbox of policies and strategies used by affordable-housing advocates.[3]

The projects profiled in *Designed for Habitat*, completed largely within the first decade of the twenty-first century, represent a fresh round of collaborations between professional designers and the affordable-housing advocacy community. Both the successes of these projects and their shortcomings provide valuable insight into the motivations and goals of these two groups and the challenges that they faced to realize these remarkable homes. The strategies that were employed in these projects provide a roadmap for how the affordable-housing advocacy community and the design community can channel their common desire to help needy families into successful collaborations.

Though there are many factors that influence the success or failure of affordable-housing initiatives, one key element is the collaboration between project partners and their ability both to understand the challenge they face and to find common ground with regard to solutions. Understanding these challenges requires a look inside the culture of both groups.

Habitat's History and Culture

The history of the affordable-housing advocacy movement in the United States has reflected the tensions between our culture's commitment to provide for the common good and our enshrinement of self-reliance and self-help: between a desire to provide well-designed and durable homes and the long-held belief that housing built with any form of assistance should not "look too good, or cost too much."[4] Habitat for Humanity, like other non-profit groups that stepped into the void created when the federal government stepped back from support for affordable housing in the mid-1970s, exemplifies these tensions.

Habitat for Humanity was founded by Millard Fuller, a successful entrepreneur, and Clarence Jordan, a Georgia farmer and biblical scholar. Jordan led a Christian community called Koinonia Farm near Americus, Georgia, that was known for its commitment to social justice, racial integration, and communal support. Fuller came to Koinonia in the mid-1960s seeking a new direction and purpose for his life. After building homes with Jordan in Georgia, and as a Christian missionary in Africa, Fuller started Habitat for Humanity in 1976, based on the idea of "partnership housing" he and Jordan had developed at Koinonia.[5] The partnership housing model was simple and compelling: "Building homes with the unpaid labor of the new homeowners and concerned volunteers, selling them at no profit and no interest, [and] recycling monthly house payments into a Fund for Humanity used to finance new construction … ."[6] Fuller's optimism, his faith, and his prodigious talent for convincing others to join his new housing ministry, helped to make Habitat for Humanity one of the largest and most successful non-profit housing development programs in the world.

Though established as a Christian housing ministry, Habitat has managed to define itself first and foremost as an organization committed to "eliminating poverty housing from the world."[7] As Jerome Baggett notes in *Habitat for Humanity: Building Private Homes, Building Public Religion*, Habitat has crafted a "minimalist, inclusive theology" that has allowed it to be very successful at attracting volunteers and significant corporate support from across the spectrum of modern society.[8]

Fuller also developed a highly effective organizational model that featured local affiliates led by community-based volunteers, and supported and guided by a central headquarters group, HFHI, based in Americus, Georgia. In the thirty-five years since its founding, HFHI has grown to include more than 1,700 affiliates, active in all fifty states in the United States. The organization also has 550 international affiliates, active in more than ninety countries. As of 2010, Habitat has built more than 350,000 houses around the world.[9]

Habitat's record of accomplishment (and its success at communications) makes the organization a natural magnet for a broad spectrum of would-be collaborators wishing to lend their time and talents to helping the organization, including architects. As illustrated by the Mockbee/Fuller exchange above, making these collaborations a success requires more than a common interest in addressing the need for good affordable housing. It also requires an understanding of how Habitat approaches design and the values and issues that shape that process.

Habitat's Approach to Home Design

Habitat affiliates are led by a volunteer board of directors, which typically has a sub-committee dedicated to the task of coordinating and overseeing the construction process of each affiliate, and to facilitating the matching of selected families with one of the affiliate's standard home design configurations. These building committees are frequently populated with volunteers from the local construction community and, occasionally, local architects.

The primary means by which Habitat maintains a home design standard is through the resources that HFHI provides to affiliates. These resources encompass a collection of affiliate manuals that include a portfolio of standard design configurations, along with associated construction details and guidelines for construction materials, construction process checklists, and so on. These templates include home designs developed by HFHI staff and designs developed by local affiliates. The HFHI headquarters staff includes a construction department that produces the design templates and construction manuals, and is dedicated to promoting a culture of building durable homes and to providing technical support, advice, and training to affiliate volunteers.

The design templates promulgated by HFHI are the most tangible representation of what "simple and decent" means to the organization. The designs emphasize efficiency over any other goal, accommodating the standard components of the program—living, eating, cooking, bathing, and sleeping—into a geometry that requires the least possible exterior surface area. HFHI's design guidelines include area limits (that is 1,050 square feet for a three-bedroom home), limits on the number of bathrooms, prohibitions against garages, requirements for a covered front entrance, and so on.

The HFHI design templates also reflect the reality that the homes will be built by unskilled volunteers. Though affiliates typically have someone experienced in construction acting as coordinator on each site, their labor force most commonly brings no prior experience to the job site. Consequently, the construction details tend towards those most simple to execute. For example, Habitat's preferred exterior cladding material is a volunteer-friendly vinyl siding, and roof slopes stay low to more safely accommodate first-time roofers. The standard designs are most typically detailed as single-family detached homes, single-story, with slab-on-grade foundations. The homes are most commonly wood-frame and clad with vinyl siding. The designs reflect a strong emphasis on maximizing material efficiency and eschew frills (such as dishwashers).

Though affiliates are free to develop their own designs, HFHI maintains a significant degree of influence on design decisions of affiliates. This is done both through direct means (such as linking access to national funding and corporate partnership programs to conformance to its standards), and through indirect means (Habitat affiliates most commonly have no other source of design advice or support). Though some affiliates have developed a high degree of sophistication in their approach to both design and construction, most are consumed with other pressures. Within the spectrum of challenges facing affiliates—organizing volunteers, raising money and soliciting donations of materials and services, screening and selecting homeowner families, and so on—developing custom design and construction solutions is beyond the reach of most affiliates.

Defining "Simple and Decent"

The design standards promoted by Habitat's headquarters group also reflect the organization's struggle to balance building the maximum possible quantity of houses with the recognized desire to build at a reasonable standard of quality ("simple and decent"). This sets up a series of tensions within the organization that translate directly to the role of design within Habitat. Chief among these are: What voice are homeowner families allowed to have with regard to defining the meaning of "simple and decent"? How should the standard of "simple and decent" change in relation to the community context of the homes? How should the goal of building homes at the lowest first cost be balanced against the long-term "occupancy cost" interests of the homeowners?

Habitat places a great deal of emphasis on the partnership established between the local volunteers who lead Habitat affiliates and serve as volunteers on construction sites, and the homeowner families the affiliate serves. Though the partnership ideal is central to the values and the theology of the organization and is no doubt sincere, these partnerships are inevitably asymmetrical. As Jerome Baggett observes, "the need for volunteers and the comparative neediness of homeowners creates a power differential between them based on social class." Habitat's espoused values are designed to guard against this imbalance. Nevertheless, as Baggett notes, "an appreciable strand of paternalism winds through the organization."[10]

In addition to an asymmetry of power, there is an asymmetry of motivation. The goal of "eliminating poverty housing" is the rallying cry for the largely middle-class volunteers who lead the affiliates and populate Habitat construction sites. Volunteering their time, resources, and energy to Habitat gives volunteers an empowering sense that they are contributing to their communities and helping to address what most see as an intractable problem. This motivation translates to a heavy emphasis on maximizing the quantity of homes built, and to a culture within affiliates where the volunteers and staff can "get caught up in the desire to build more and more houses."[11] In this context, any initiative seen as making homes more complicated to build (such as adapting to neighborhood context or using more durable materials) comes under fire—remember Fuller's "lottery for humanity" comment noted earlier.

Though Habitat's requirement that homeowners contribute time to building homes for other families serves to kindle a sense of community responsibility in homeowners, obtaining the best home possible is, first and foremost, their primary goal and the primary source of their empowerment in the "partnership."

These disparities in power and motivation can be manifest at many stages of the process, from family screening and selection to the choice of home location and home design. As Baggett notes, homeowners report feeling pressured to "move boldly into neighborhoods that are often located in reputedly dangerous (and thus relatively inexpensive) urban areas and transform them, simply by behaving as empowered and law-abiding citizens."[12] In most affiliates, homeowner families have a relatively narrow range of involvement in the key committees, including those that set design and construction standards for the affiliate. Prospective homeowners also have limited latitude in revising the design of the home templates offered them by the affiliate beyond tailoring the number of bedrooms and making minor interior changes.[13]

As several of the case studies illustrate, this relegation of the homeowner to the sidelines of the design-shaping process is a common source of conflict for architects, who are trained to tailor designs as closely as possible to end user needs.

Responding to Community Context

Another problem that Habitat has wrestled with is the tension created when it encounters resistance from communities and neighborhoods to the construction of homes that run counter to local home values and design character.

This tension activates two powerful tenets of Habitat's core values: the position that the organization should stand in resistance to the creeping affluence of modern society and build homes that express a "critical perspective towards the market," and the belief that Habitat's goal to build meaningful and sustainable partnerships within the wider communities where they work renders concessions to local standards justifiable.[14] This latter position also echoes the prevailing wisdom within the larger affordable-housing advocacy community, gained from the painful experience of failed projects of the 1950s and 1960s, that "above all, affordable housing should not look different from market-rate housing."[15]

As several of the projects analyzed in this book illustrate, there is evidence that the "community partnership" perspective is gaining traction within Habitat, and that the effort to reconcile the modest budgets of Habitat homes with designs that accommodate neighborhood context is one of the key factors that motivate Habitat affiliates to partner with professional designers.

Production versus Performance

Habitat has also experienced a significant transition in its understanding of the relationship between the benefits of minimizing construction cost (in order to optimize productivity and lower purchase cost) and the often negative impact of these choices on long-term occupancy costs for Habitat homeowners. Unlike the model used by commercial home builders, Habitat's financing model and its organizational values establish relatively long-term relationships between homeowners and the organization. Many affiliates are still engaged with homeowner families beyond the lifespan of the inexpensive construction materials favored by the organization (such as vinyl siding and asphalt shingles). This extended engagement with homeowners has made Habitat more sensitive to the burden associated with replacing short-lived materials and open to consideration of more durable material choices, and to design solutions that make the replacement of major equipment and systems easier.

Perhaps the most significant shift toward consideration of occupancy cost over construction cost has been Habitat's embrace of design and construction strategies aimed at lowering energy costs for homeowners. It is not uncommon for monthly energy expenses to be comparable to a Habitat homeowner's mortgage payment, and escalating energy costs pose a significant threat to their financial security. HFHI's construction department staff have been pushing affiliates to adopt the EPA's Energy Star standards for home construction for more than a decade, and have developed significant corporate sponsorships aimed at providing affiliates with energy-efficient materials and appliances at low cost and at providing affiliate training and support.[16] As with the challenge of community-responsive home designs, developing design solutions that extend energy performance beyond the materials and systems and into home configuration has also been a catalyst for partnerships between affiliates and architects.

Architects and Affordable Housing

The history of the architecture community's involvement in the affordable-housing movement in the United States is primarily centered on multi-family housing and on urban settings. The record of affordable housing designed by architects reflects dramatic shifts in strategy and outcomes, tied to dramatic shifts in political support for publicly subsidized, affordable housing. Though there were a few notable successes in the first half of the twentieth century, the profession's primary turn at shaping affordable housing in the United States—the slum-clearing initiatives and large public housing projects of the 1950s and 1960s—proved disastrous.[17] Among the many consequences of the high-profile failures of both policy and design in this period was the near exile of architects from the national dialogue on housing policy.

Charles Bohl describes 1970 to 1990 as the period of "Design in Exile," where "the manner in which assisted housing had been planned and designed was being cast as part of the problem rather than part of the solution. In fact, planning and design in general were being widely attacked and discredited as a means for improving living conditions and resolving social problems."[18]

Despite this setback, architects remained engaged in the development of affordable housing throughout the latter decades of the twentieth century. The focus of this work shifted from large, high-rise developments to low-rise projects of medium to high density built initially with federal support and subsequently (after the federal programs were suspended in 1973) with non-profit community development corporations (CDCs) as their clients.[19] The body of work at this scale produced by architects over the last few decades has been much more success-ful, largely because it reflects a design process that is responsive to the complex influences of end users, public authorities, neighborhood groups, and community interests. The work of Michael Pyatok exemplifies the best of this approach.[20]

Affordable-housing advocates largely agree that the development of well-designed multi-family, medium- to high-density housing is the most reasonable and environmentally sustainable way to meet the mushrooming need for housing in the United States. Though programs like the Federal Housing Administration (FHA) mortgage insurance programs and "billions of dollars in Community Development Block Grants and HOME Investment Partnership Programs" now support afford-able homeownership programs in communities across the United States, the scale of need far outstrips current production.[21] In this context, many argue that archi-tects must do more than offer their design expertise. Robert Gutman, like many within the profession, argues that "architects must adopt an advocacy role ... [and] engage in political action that will encourage the expansion of government pro-grams that underwrite low-income housing production."[22]

Though multi-family housing is the area of greatest need, development at this scale is largely beyond the capacity of the many small CDCs and non-profit groups that are still the primary actors in the affordable-housing arena within the United States. Habitat for Humanity affiliates have begun to explore ways to adapt their model to higher-density development, but their focus remains on single-family homes and on the economic and social empowerment that home ownership bestows on their homeowner clients. Architects who aspire to collaborate with Habitat will have to be skilled at working at this scale and adept at working within the modest budgets that come with this market. Unfortunately, there are not many architects who have developed both credentials.

Single-family detached homes dominate the US housing market, accounting for more than 62 percent of the total homes in the US Census Department's 2007 American Housing Survey.[23] Almost 78 percent of these homes are owner-occupied. As Gutman observes, this has been a market where nearly eighty years of effort by the American Institute of Architects to "bring architectural services to the middle class home buyer" has been largely unsuccessful. Though consensus on the involvement of architects in this market is hard to find, the conventional wisdom is that a very small percentage of this market reflects the work of professionally trained architects.[24] More directly to the issue of *affordable single-family homes*, the American Institute of Architects reports that only 6 percent of its member firms report involvement in this market sector.[25]

The relative absence of architects in the affordable single-family home building sector translates to very little current experience within the profession of the difficult and challenging assignment of designing for this market. Though most architects will assert that their experience at larger scales of building can translate to this sector, there are, nonetheless, often significant differences in the ways architects and affordable-housing advocates, like Habitat for Humanity, view the goals of these projects. These differences often make for friction and frustration when they seek to collaborate.

To make these collaborations more successful, the architects and the non-profits they serve must find a way to frame their dialogue about design goals and design process in such a way as to embrace the values and perspectives of both groups. This challenge, and the means by which the project teams profiled in this book have met it, is the primary focus of *Designed for Habitat: Collaborations with Habitat for Humanity*.

The chapters that follow profile the results of thirteen successful collaborations between Habitat for Humanity affiliates and two key communities within the architectural profession: schools of architecture and practicing architects. The cases represent projects from across the United States, and from across the full spectrum of Habitat for Humanity affiliates—from large urban affiliates to small affiliates based in rural communities. They also illustrate a broad range of design objectives that draw the partners together, including improved energy efficiency, exploring innovative construction strategies, responding to site context, and investigating the potentials of innovative approaches to the design and construction.

Despite the constraints of cost, delivery, and financing associated with Habitat for Humanity's project framework, each of these partnerships has resulted in homes of remarkable design quality. We hope that understanding how these projects came about will help design professions and affordable-housing advocates who aspire to achieve similar results.

GROUP

ONE

COLLABORATIONS WITH ARCHITECTURE SCHOOLS

Chapter 1

DESIGNhabitat 2

Greensboro, Alabama

Auburn University and Habitat for Humanity® Hale County (AL)

Key Partnerships

David Hinson and Stacy Norman, Auburn University School of Architecture (AU)

Karen McCauley, executive director, Alabama Association of Habitat Affiliates (AAHA)

Steven Brown, executive director, Habitat for Humanity Troup/Chambers County (GA & AL) (HFHTC)

Greg Peet, Palm Harbor Homes, Inc. (DESIGNhabitat 2.0)

Kevin Law, Nationwide Custom Homes (DESIGNhabitat 2.1)

Pamela Dorr, executive director, Habitat for Humanity Hale County (AL) (HFHHC)

Program Summary

DESIGNhabitat 2.0 home

3-bedroom, 1-bath, single-family detached home

1,100 square feet

DESIGNhabitat 2.1 home

3-bedroom, 2-bath, single-family detached home

1,225 square feet

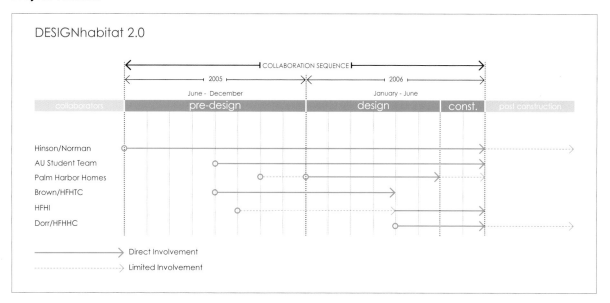

Catalysts for Collaboration

In the spring of 2001, professor David Hinson of Auburn University's School of Architecture was approached by Design Alabama (a non-profit working to promote design in the state) with the prospect of helping Habitat develop new home design standards. Design Alabama staff introduced Hinson to Karen McCauley, executive director of the Alabama Association of Habitat Affiliates (AAHA), the coordinating state support organization for Alabama's thirty-five Habitat affiliates. According to Hinson, he and McCauley "hit it off from the start" and began crafting a structure for a partnership between Auburn and AAHA.

They came up with a plan whereby Hinson and students from the architecture program would explore new approaches to design of Habitat homes with the goals of lowering homeowner operating and maintenance costs, and developing designs that would, as Hinson describes, "respond to the climate, context, and culture" of Alabama communities. With approval and support from the AAHA board, the DESIGNhabitat program was begun.[1]

In the first cycle of their collaborations with AAHA (2001–02), Hinson and his students designed and built the DESIGNhabitat 1 home in partnership with the Lee County (AL) Habitat affiliate.[2] This home featured a prominent screened porch on the street side of the house, an emphasis on natural ventilation, efficient mechanical systems, and, as Hinson describes it, "a vocabulary of design details that make the house feel like it belongs in the early twentieth-century neighborhood where it was built." Over the next two years, four derivations of this prototype design were built by Habitat affiliates in other communities. Hinson and his students provided support for these projects in the form of construction drawings and advice regarding the energy conservation features of the design.

In 2004, Hinson learned that small, often rural, affiliates (like many in Alabama) faced significant challenges trying to build homes despite having small pools of volunteer-builders to draw on. This prompted Hinson to begin investigating off-site prefabrication as a means of helping these affiliates build more homes. Hinson and his students studied a wide range of prefabrication strategies and concluded that a modular approach—constructing whole sections of the home in a factory and assembling them on-site—offered the most potential to address the problem.

In 2005, Hinson approached McCauley and the AAHA board with a proposal to test the viability of this approach via "DESIGNhabitat 2," a second round of student design and construction patterned after the 2001–02 collaboration. With approval from the AAHA board, Hinson and McCauley worked through the summer of 2005 to line up the partners for the project.

Design Process

With help from the state association representing the modular builder industry, Hinson secured a commitment from Palm Harbor Homes, one of the nation's largest manufacturers of modular and HUD-Code homes (aka "mobile homes"), to build the modular sections of the house in their North Alabama plant.

McCauley lined up support from Habitat for Humanity Troup/Chambers County (HFHTC), based about a half-hour drive away from the Auburn campus. HFHTC agreed to provide funding for the home (equal to their standard budget), to provide the lot for the home, and to select the homeowner family. Hinson and McCauley secured support from a private foundation to underwrite the anticipated cost premium associated with a modular approach.

In the fall semester of 2005, Hinson and Stacy Norman (a local architect and adjunct faculty member at Auburn) began a fifteen-week "pre-design research" seminar with a team of sixteen students from the architecture program. The aim of this seminar was to immerse the students in the design standards and production methods associated with modular fabrication and, as Hinson explained, "to explore just how innovative this approach to construction could be." The semester involved visits by the students to Palm Harbor's plant and meetings with Palm Harbor's design and production staff to learn the opportunities and limits of their construction process. The students also studied the range of design strategies and approaches used by professional architects and academic design programs to explore the design potentials of prefabricated construction.

Less than a month into the fall term, Hurricanes Katrina and Rita devastated the Gulf Coast region and brought a dramatic shift in the context for the project. The storms and their aftermath devastated a four-state region, including the western counties of Alabama. Overnight, the crisis that had given impetus to the project—insufficient volunteer-builder resources—became the biggest problem facing Habitat affiliates across the south. Late in the fall term, leaders of "Operation Home Delivery," the program set up by Habitat for Humanity International to coordinate their hurricane response efforts, visited with the Auburn team and asked the group to consider how their work might be applied to Habitat's rebuilding efforts.

At the conclusion of the semester, the students presented a summary of their research to the staff at Palm Harbor and to the HFHTC board, along with an outline of their planned approach to the next phase of the project.

Hinson and Norman planned the 2006 spring semester to begin with an intense five-week design phase. Students worked in teams to develop a range of design solutions, which were gradually narrowed to five options. The students had determined that the width and length standards for modular unit production and transportation suggested that the program of spaces in the home could be accommodated in two prefabricated modules, and each design proposal featured a different approach to configuring these units and different strategies for the scope of on-site construction.

In mid-February Hinson and Norman assembled a "super jury" made up of representatives from Palm Harbor, the AAHA board, Steve Brown (executive director of HFHTC), and faculty from Auburn to review the students' proposed designs and to select one solution for construction. After hearing presentations by each student team and reviewing the drawings and models, the jury selected a scheme featuring two factory-built modules connected by a site-built center bay. This scheme featured a distinctive "butterfly" roof configuration over the site-built center section, and emphasized a very simple and efficient plan configuration. The hybrid nature of this scheme (two-thirds prefabricated/one-third site-built) also appealed to the concerns of the Habitat representatives on the jury that the modular approach would leave too little work for homeowners and community volunteers to build. According to Hinson, "the jury felt [the selected scheme] would satisfy Habitat's 'sweat equity' emphasis. They really wanted opportunities to preserve the role of homeowners and community volunteers in the construction process."

Immediately after the super jury, the students began to work closely with Palm Harbor to refine the design and plan out the construction of the house, and with HFHTC to refine the design for construction on a site in nearby Chambers County.

At about the mid-point of the semester, Hinson and Norman received notice from Steve Brown that the chair of the HFHTC board had "concerns about the design." The board chair (an architect) had been unable to participate in the super jury and had alerted Brown that "he was not comfortable with this direction," recounted Hinson. The HFHTC board chair visited the school to discuss the project with Hinson and Norman and it soon became clear that the problem was serious. "It was clear that he had real problems with the design," according to Hinson, especially the butterfly roof configuration over the center bay. After a series of meetings and modifications to the design aimed at finding a compromise solution, the HFHTC board chair and the Auburn team reached an impasse. The following week Brown notified Hinson that HFHTC was withdrawing its support for the project. Suddenly, it appeared DESIGNhabitat 2.0 was over. "That was a shock to all of us," notes Hinson. "It looked like the project was dead."

In an effort to save the project, Hinson and Norman enlisted help from Karen McCauley and her contacts across the state. "It felt like we spent most of the next forty-eight hours on the phone," said Hinson, "but it paid off." By the end of the week McCauley had lined up both a new affiliate partner—the newly formed Habitat for Humanity Hale County affiliate (HFHHC), and a new project sponsor—Operation Home Delivery.

Hale County was one of the Alabama counties raked by the eastern edge of the hurricane, and the recently formed Hale County affiliate had yet to build its first home. According to Pamela Dorr, executive director of the affiliate, the HFHHC board was initially skeptical about utilizing the modular approach, but "we were won over by the energy, knowledge, and commitment of the students and faculty."

Construction Process

The Auburn team quickly regrouped to adapt their construction strategy to coordinate with the new affiliate partner and to the new site in Greensboro, Alabama—three hours away from Auburn's campus. The new location—too far from Auburn for daily commutes—meant that the students could not begin construction until spring classes concluded, resulting in a very narrow window of time before other summer commitments would dissolve the team. In consultation with Hinson and Norman, the students came up with an ambitious plan to compete the on-site phase of the project in fifteen days, beginning right after the last day of classes. They would use the balance of the term to refine the details of the design, build full-scale mockups of key construction details, and fabricate the kitchen cabinets in Auburn's on-campus woodworking shop. As the semester drew to a close the affiliate completed site clearing and installed the foundations, while Palm Harbor put the modular units into production.

"The first full day on site was an amazing thing," observed Hinson. "The two modules arrived via truck about mid-morning, and by lunch two-thirds of the home rested on the foundation." As the crane crew departed, the Auburn team began framing the center section. In addition to building the center connecting bay and porches, the students planned to sheath the modules on-site, install the kitchen cabinets, and complete the interior trim finishes for the home. "We worked twelve-hour days for two weeks," notes Hinson, "rain or shine." The homeowner and her children, forced to vacate their rental home due to storm damage, worked alongside the Auburn team on many days, along with a few local HFHHC volunteers. At the conclusion of the two-week "blitz" the house was substantially complete, with a few unfinished areas of interior work, and some painting and utility connections to finish. HFHHC completed these items over the next month and in mid-June the Auburn team returned to Greensboro to see the house dedicated and turned over to the homeowner family.

Lessons Learned

From Hinson's perspective, the DESIGNhabitat 2 project offered a number of lessons.[3] Foremost, according to Hinson, was the impact of the experience on the students' understanding of affordable-housing design and the challenges associated with exploring new construction technologies. "We took a very serious approach to this as a design-based research project," notes Hinson. "We knew Habitat was keenly interested in modular construction because of Katrina, and we wanted to demonstrate the design potential of this approach and test the cost versus on-site labor question. I think we accomplished both," said Hinson.

As anticipated, the construction costs for the house were about $68 per square foot (a 23 percent cost premium over a traditional volunteer-built Habitat house completed in similar areas in the state), largely because the modular process requires a for-profit entity (the modular producer) to build a substantial portion of the home. On the other hand, the house was completed much faster and with fewer on-site volunteer hours than the norm for an affiliate the size of HFHHC.

DESIGNhabitat 2.1, a second modular home, was designed and built in 2008 by Auburn students (led by Hinson and Norman) in collaboration with HFHHC and Nationwide Custom Homes, a modular home producer based in Arabi, Georgia.

The combined perspective gained from these two homes gave the Auburn team and AAHA valuable perspective on the role of modular construction in situations like those faced by Habitat in the wake of the 2005 hurricanes. "An affiliate would not use this approach if it had adequate volunteers to build conventionally," observes Hinson, "but when faced with limited volunteers, we confirmed that modular is a viable approach." Operation Home Delivery has made significant use of modular construction in its post-Katrina rebuilding efforts.[4]

The withdrawal of HFHTC also illustrated the risks of pursuing an ambitious design approach without securing commitment from all the key stakeholders within an affiliate. It also taught the Auburn team that a wide range of attitudes about design can be found within any affiliate board. "We really thought we had designed a pretty inclusive process for getting everyone on board," observed Hinson, "but learned it only takes one key stakeholder being out of the loop to turn the project upside down."

From Dorr's perspective, the biggest lessons of the project rested in the way it expanded the young affiliate's capacity to build high-quality homes. In the early stages of creating the affiliate, Dorr and the affiliate board had assumed there would be an ample supply of home designs to choose from, but according to Dorr, "it was ridiculously hard to find something we wanted to build." The partnership with Auburn taught the affiliate how to leverage the expertise of outside groups to speed up their learning process. "We learned more [about design] from that first project than we would have by building twenty homes on our own," notes Dorr.

The homeowner and community response to the project has been very positive, according to Dorr. "The thing we were most surprised about was how many people travel here to see that house," says Dorr. "It has become a source of pride in our community. We never expected to have something so remarkable."

The DESIGNhabitat 2 project has earned an array of awards, ranging from state and national awards for housing design to awards for teaching and community engagement. The partnership between Auburn and AAHA continues to produce new rounds of design-based research collaborations, including DESIGNhabitat 3, profiled in Chapter 4.

diagram of site-built middle bay and modular bays

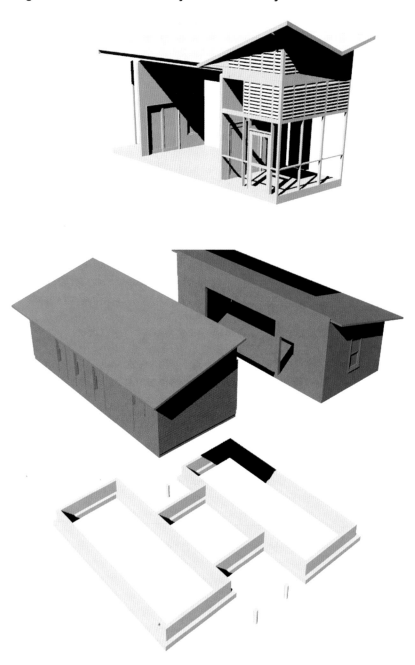

modular bay in production

setting of module on foundation

view from street

DESIGNhabitat 2.0 floor plan

Key

1 - Living
2 - Dining
3 - Kitchen
4 - Bedroom
5 - Bath
6 - Porch

1'   5'   10'   20'

living space showing vaulted ceiling

DESIGNhabitat 2.1 floor plan

Key

1 - Living
2 - Dining
3 - Kitchen
4 - Porch
5 - Bath
6 - Bedroom

1'   5'   10'   20'

diagram of modules and site-built front porch

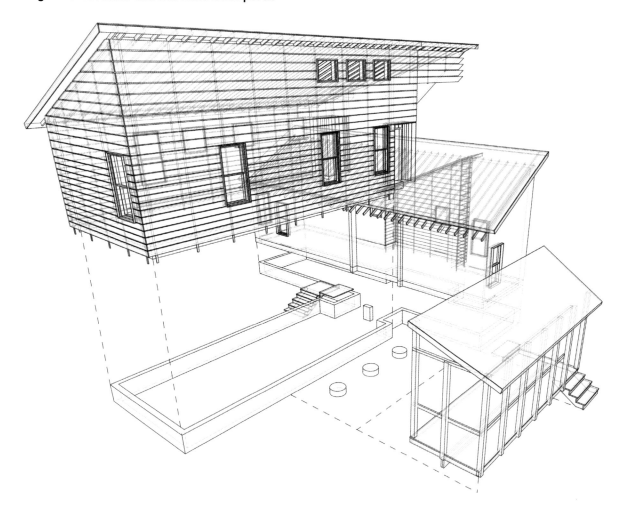

view of entry porch from street

view from rear

Chapter 2

Habitat Trails

Rogers, Arkansas

University of Arkansas Community Design Center and Habitat for Humanity® Benton County (AR)

Key Partnerships

Stephen Luoni and Aaron Gabriel, University of Arkansas Community Design Center (UACDC)

Marty Matlock, professor of Ecological Engineering, University of Arkansas

Debbie Wieneke and Pat Adams, Habitat for Humanity Benton County (HFHBC)

Program Summary

Urban prototype home

3-bedroom, 2-bath, single-family detached home

1,250 square feet

Project Timeline

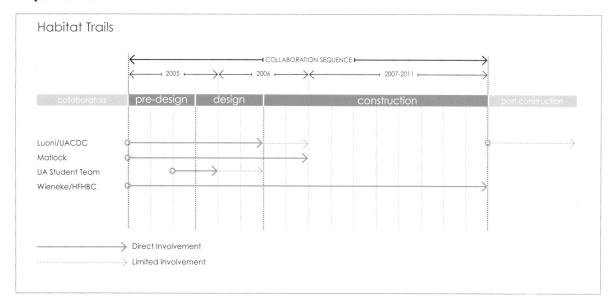

Catalysts for Collaboration

In the spring of 2005 Debbie Wieneke, executive director of the HFHBC affiliate, along with Bill Adams and Pat Adams from the HFHBC board, became aware that the owners of a five-acre parcel of land on the edge of Rogers, Arkansas, a small but growing community near Fayetteville (home to the University of Arkansas), were interested in selling the land if they could find a buyer interested in developing the property in an ecologically sensitive manner. With the help of a grant from the Walton Family Foundation (based in nearby Bentonville), HFHBC acquired the land with the understanding, notes Wieneke, that the affiliate would incorporate sustainable development strategies and "approach the project in an innovative way."

The UACDC operates as a non-profit design center providing design and planning services to communities across Arkansas.[1] Affiliated with the School of Architecture at the University of Arkansas, the UACDC allows architecture students to gain hands-on experience working on projects under the direction of the center's professional staff.

Stephen Luoni, director of the UACDC, and Marty Matlock, from the university's Ecological Engineering department, had been looking for an opportunity to partner on a project that would introduce the ecologically based stormwater management technologies associated with "low-impact development" (LID) to Northwest Arkansas. When Matlock and Luoni learned of the HFHBC land acquisition they contacted the affiliate and offered their help, and worked with Wieneke through the summer to plan their collaboration. In the summer of 2005, the UACDC signed a two-year design services agreement with HFHBC to develop a design strategy for the project.

Design Process

Luoni and Matlock organized a UACDC design team that included Aaron Gabriel and students from the architecture and ecological engineering programs at the university. As the fall semester of 2005 began, the team began a simultaneous effort to develop an innovation site plan approach and designs for the homes that would integrate with and reinforce the site design strategies.

Working closely with Wieneke and Adams, the UACDC team identified several key design goals for the project including the management of stormwater runoff via features of the site landscape rather than the conventional "curb–gutter–pipe" strategies common to development in the area. They also sought to preserve a significant portion of the site as commonly held open space to both facilitate the ecological functions of the design and provide a physical "commons" that would knit the individual homes into a community of neighbors. Lastly, the team proposed design solutions for the street systems and individual homes.

Wieneke and Adams were excited by the new approach and eager to see if the strategies could be realized (as Matlock and Luoni assured them) at a lower cost than a conventional site infrastructure approach.

The central features of the design that emerged over the course of the fall of 2005 were a dramatic departure from the affiliate's prior experience with multi-unit site design. Rather than subdividing the entire site into individual parcels, the site design reserves over a third of the property as open space shared by all homeowners. The central feature of the scheme is a "commons" at the center of the site, wrapped by a single-loaded street. Eleven of the site's seventeen planned units face this commons area. The streets are intentionally narrow (to "calm" the traffic) and are lined with bioswales and "stormwater gardens" designed to direct stormwater to a one-acre "wet meadow" (replacing the conventional retention pond) at the low (west) end of the site. Mark Boyer, a faculty colleague from Arkansas's Landscape Architecture department, helped Matlock and Luoni select the plant materials (soft rushes, St John's Wort, sweet bay magnolias, and other native plants) integral to the "ecological infrastructure" of the bioswales, street side gardens and wet meadow.

As the site design strategy took shape, UACDC staff and architecture students worked to develop a set of house designs that would complement the overall design for the neighborhood. The result of the student effort was a portfolio of eight unit designs for the seventeen homes planned for the site, covering eleven single-family detached units and three duplexes. The majority of the homes would be the ten homes arrayed around the central open space.

The prototype designs for these ten homes were dubbed the "Bungalow" and the "Urban Vernacular." Each design featured large front porches facing the commons and street, serving to reinforce the connections between each home and the shared community spaces. The designs for the Urban Vernacular scheme (slated to be the first house constructed) featured two-story plans with double-height living areas. In a departure from the Habitat norm, the unit designs featured covered carports (required by the City of Rogers), which were integrated with the front porches to give the units a larger look and feel across the large open space of the central commons.

From the outset of the project, Wieneke and the UACDC team knew that the project would face a complicated approvals process. Habitat Trails would be the first example of low-impact development in the area, and the site design features would require variances from the community's existing development standards for street construction and stormwater control.

Understanding that buy-in from officials from the local community would be crucial, the UACDC team began working with the Rogers municipal authorities, including the fire marshal and representatives from the public works department, to ensure that they would support the project. Wieneke also began working with the local news media to generate public interest and support for the project.

At the conclusion of the fall design phase, the design proposals were unveiled at a public reception hosted by the affiliate, and the scheme received lots of positive responses from the community and media. This created, according to

Wieneke, "valuable good will and momentum" for the project prior to the permitting phase.

Beginning in January of 2006, the team worked to develop the detailed engineering documentation needed to secure approvals for the project and provide the requisite direction for the construction team. Wieneke and Adams credit the UACDC team's efforts to thoroughly explain how each design feature would perform—supported by successful examples from other areas of the country—with the city's acceptance of the project. According to Wieneke and Adams, the thoroughness of the UACDC's preparations, coupled with Luoni's assertions that "these concepts are new but they will work," convinced the City of Rogers to grant more than thirty variances to their site development ordinances and approve the project.

Construction Process

With approvals in hand, the team faced the challenge of finding a local contractor to construct the innovative features of the site design. After initial efforts to find a local contractor to take on the site work failed to attract anyone willing to do the unfamiliar work at a reasonable cost, HFHBC board member Pat Adams (who owned a site work company) agreed to take on the project and, according to Luoni, proved to be "a great partner" in the process.

Luoni and Matlock knew that their construction documentation for the site work would have to be both thorough and detailed—much more so than had they proposed a system familiar to the local construction community. For example, since all of the stormwater collection would occur above ground (rather than in conventional underground pipes), the design team provided highly detailed grading plans to Adams to make sure the stormwater collection system would be properly constructed. In another example of the unique nature of the design, Luoni noted that the Habitat Trails design required a different approach to landscape material choices. "No plant is decorative, every plant is infrastructure," Luoni said, explaining that the plant material played a crucial role in filtering pollutants out of the water running off of paved areas. Consequently, few of the specified native plants selected for this role were available through local sources. To make sure the right materials were used, Luoni and Matlock found nurseries outside the local area who could supply the specified plants for the project.

Though Adams agreed that there were quite a few "learning curves" associated with this new approach, the cost savings projections of Matlock and Luoni were borne out. According to Adams, "we found we could build [site infrastructure] this way for 20 percent less cost than our traditional approach."

Though the site design proved to be a big success, the collaboration between the UACDC and the affiliate on the design and construction of the first house did not work out so well. Though Wieneke and other representatives from the affiliate had been involved with the UACDC team during the design phase for the houses, features of the UACDC design for the first house to be built (the Urban Vernacular prototype), such as the double-height spaces over the living areas and steep roof pitches, proved difficult for the affiliate to build with unskilled volunteers.

To compound the challenge faced on the first house, HFHBC made the decision to build the exterior walls and roof of the first house with a Structural Insulated Panel System (SIPS) after the UACDC team had produced construction documents based on a traditional framing approach. As the affiliate rushed to complete the house in time to meet a funding deadline, efforts to correct the misinterpretations of the design drawings became an increasingly frustrating experience for both the affiliate and the UACDC staff. These changes led to cost overruns and strained relationships between the project partners.

According to Luoni, the rapport between the UACDC and HFHBC was also strained by a turnover of leadership on the affiliate board. In his view, some of these new board members, who were not involved in the initial design phase, were "cool to the project," and expressed the view that the Habitat Trails design standards developed by the UACDC were "too extravagant."

Efforts by Wieneke and Luoni to realign the affiliate's goals and those of the UACDC after the first home was completed were not successful. Reluctantly, according to Luoni, both agreed that efforts to collaborate on subsequent stages of home construction would be "unproductive."

Though the five additional homes built by the affiliate to date have not been UACDC designs, Wieneke noted that the affiliate has "tried to follow the principles of the plan" in as many ways as possible. The affiliate has built two additional homes in Habitat Trails based on modified versions of the Bungalow prototype. According to Wieneke these units incorporate many features of the UACDC design, such as extending the gable roof form over the carports and large porches on the front of each home, but have been "simplified to make them more volunteer-friendly."

In addition to the challenge of the new construction methods associated with the project, the affiliate recognized that they would have to develop new tools to help the homeowners manage the shared spaces of the Habitat Trails neighborhood. Both the affiliate board and the City of Rogers had expressed concerns over how the common areas would be maintained. In response, the affiliate developed a "property owners association" (which collects $25 a month from each homeowner to manage these areas) and Wieneke stays very involved with the homeowner families to be sure they understand the differences between Habitat Trails and a conventional subdivision. "We give prospective homeowners the choice to 'opt in' to this neighborhood," reports Wieneke. "When the family selection committee has picked a family [for this neighborhood], we bring the family in and set them down and explain the ecological-neighborhood concept." Consequently, notes Wieneke, the families who choose to live in Habitat Trails are committed to the shared responsibilities that come with this site.

Lessons Learned

The Habitat Trails project has earned eleven awards for its innovative development approach, receiving accolades from organizations ranging from professional design societies to the National Science Foundation. According to Wieneke, the project remains a source of pride for the Benton County affiliate and a "best-practice benchmark" of how affordable housing developers can successfully integrate low-impact development strategies into their approach. Both Wieneke and Luoni report that the project attracts a steady stream of municipal officials, developers, and Habitat leaders eager to study the project, mirror its details, and learn from the affiliate's experience in both building the project and managing its phased implementation.

The Habitat Trails case provides a compelling roadmap for affiliates and design teams interested in pursuing sustainable goals at the neighborhood scale, both in terms of the design strategies employed and the degree of special effort required by design teams to get non-traditional approaches through the community approvals process and see them constructed properly.

In addition to the site development cost savings and the conservation benefits realized in this project, Habitat Trails also illustrates that an "affordable" neighborhood can provide individual homeowners with an "amenity-rich" community. The open spaces created via the central commons, the wildflower meadow, the walking trails, and the common playground and gazebo are all possible because of this focus on shared common spaces over private yards.

The Habitat Trails project also illustrates that the aspirations of design teams can easily outdistance even the most "innovation-friendly" Habitat affiliate when the rationale for innovation does not mesh with the affiliates' core goals.

In the case of Habitat Trails, the design innovation of the site design approach was underpinned by an ethic of environmental responsibility and the prospect of lower cost—goals that aligned well with the core mission and objectives of the affiliate. This alignment of values and goals—so successful on the site design challenge—broke down when the UACDC team turned to the home designs. Here, each innovative feature of the homes—from the large porches and double-height living areas to unfamiliar construction technologies—seemed to create hurdles for the affiliate, hurdles that they could (ultimately) not overcome.

site plan

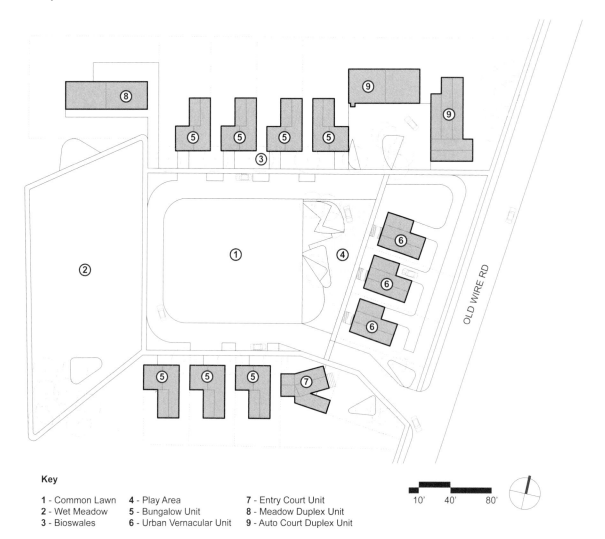

Key

1 - Common Lawn   4 - Play Area   7 - Entry Court Unit
2 - Wet Meadow   5 - Bungalow Unit   8 - Meadow Duplex Unit
3 - Bioswales   6 - Urban Vernacular Unit   9 - Auto Court Duplex Unit

10'   40'   80'

diagram of LID design features

"Up to 47 percent of surface pollutants can be removed in the first 15 minutes of a storm event, including pesticides, fertilizers and biologically derived materials and litter...Providing pervious surfaces that capture stormwater runoff increases opportunities for pollutant removal and attenuation of flow velocity."

Portland Metro: *Green Streets: Innovative Solutions for Stormwater and Stream Crossings*

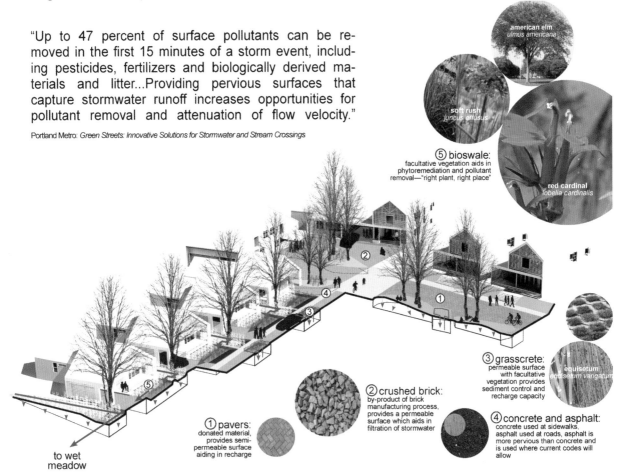

american elm
ulmus americana

soft rush
juncus effusus

⑤ bioswale:
facultative vegetation aids in phytoremediation and pollutant removal—"right plant, right place"

red cardinal
lobelia cardinalis

③ grasscrete:
permeable surface with facultative vegetation provides sediment control and recharge capacity

equisetum
equisetum variegatum

② crushed brick:
by-product of brick manufacturing process, provides a permeable surface which aids in filtration of stormwater

④ concrete and asphalt:
concrete used at sidewalks, asphalt used at roads, asphalt is more pervious than concrete and is used where current codes will allow

① pavers:
donated material, provides semi-permeable surface aiding in recharge

to wet meadow

view of common lawn from wet meadow

view of pervious paths and native vegetation

view from wet meadow

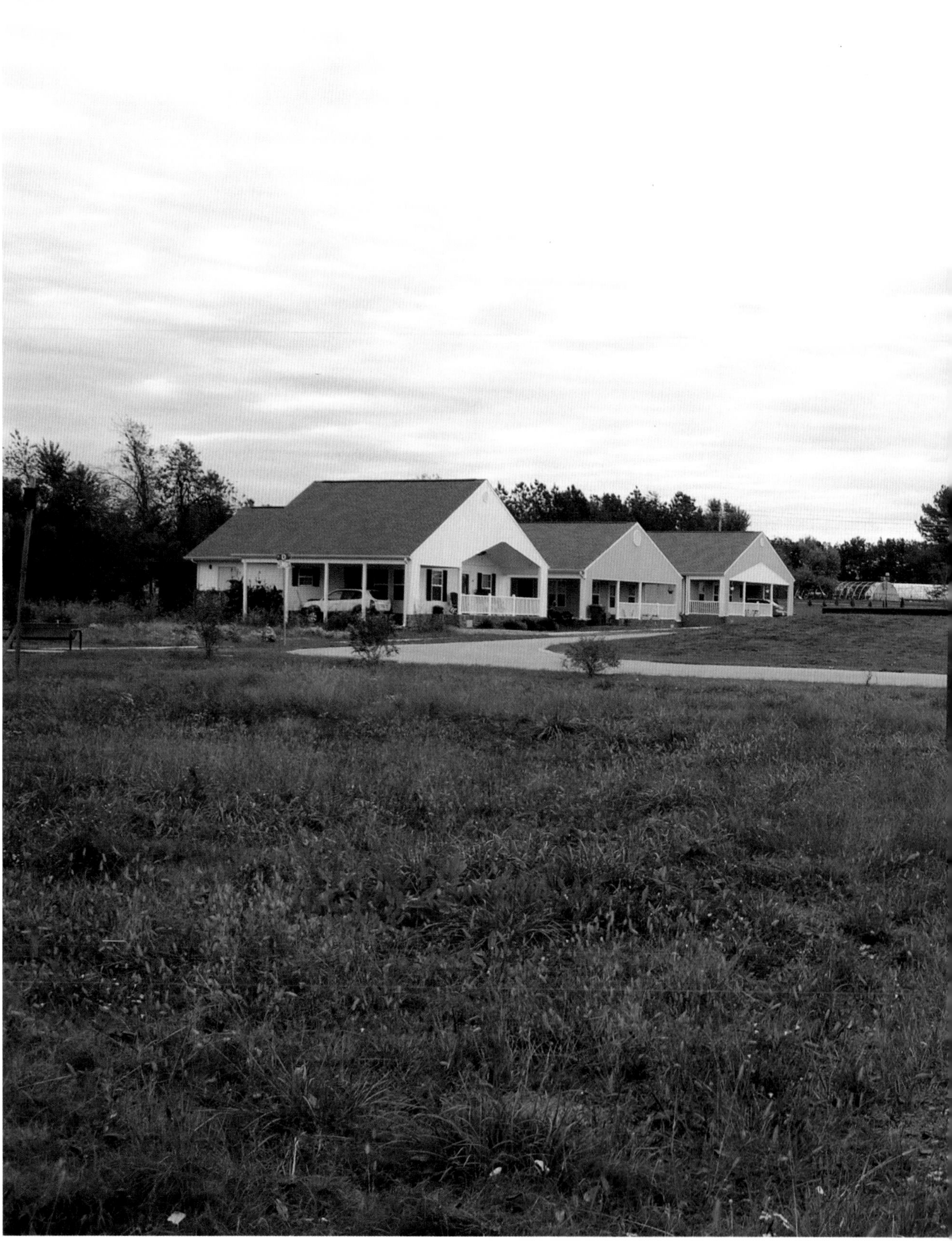

floor plan of Urban Vernacular unit

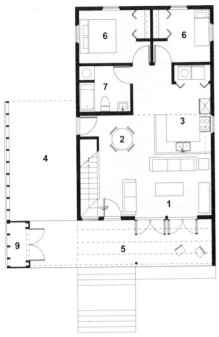

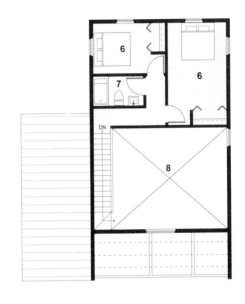

Ground Floor

Second Floor

Key

1 - Living   **4** - Carport   **7** - Bath

2 - Dining   **5** - Porch   **8** - Open to Below

3 - Kitchen   **6** - Bedroom   **9** - Storage

1'   5'   10'   20'

proposed street view

view of completed Urban Vernacular home

Left elevation

Front elevation

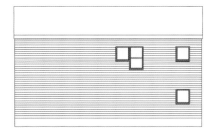

Right elevation

view of first completed house

Chapter 3

VPH House

Baton Rouge, Louisiana
LSU School of Architecture and Habitat for Humanity® Greater Baton Rouge (LA)

Key Partnerships

David Conrath, Louisiana State University College of Art and Design

David Baird, Louisiana State University School of Architecture (LSUSA)

Ann Ruble, executive director, Habitat for Humanity Greater Baton Rouge (HFHBR)

Mark Montgomery, volunteer project manager, Habitat for Humanity Greater Baton Rouge (HFHBR)

Lynn Clark, executive director, Habitat for Humanity Greater Baton Rouge (HFHBR)

The Vinyl Institute (Vinyl Products Manufacturers Association)

Program Summary

3-bedroom, 2-bath, single-family detached home

1,275 square feet

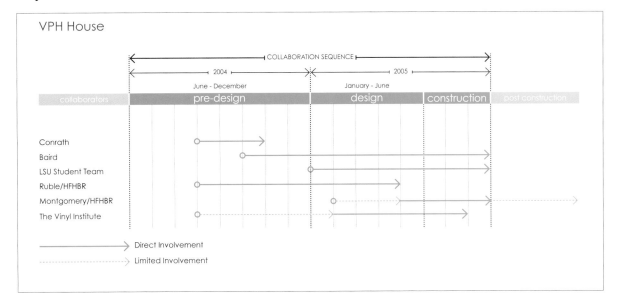

Catalysts for Collaboration

In the fall of 2004, the Vinyl Institute, the trade association representing vinyl product manufacturers in the United States, was nearing the end of its 'Vinyl Partners for Habitat' campaign, a five-year, $1-million commitment to build Habitat homes in Baton Rouge, Louisiana. As part of the final stage of the campaign, HFHBR's new executive director, Ann Ruble, and Dean David Conrath of LSU's College of Art and Design developed a plan to have a group of LSU architecture students design and build a Habitat home in their final (fifth-year) design studio. The collaboration received additional funding support from the Vinyl Institute, including funds to support cash prizes for the student design competition that would occur in the first phase of the studio. Conrath assigned professor David Baird to lead the studio, which would commence the following January.

Design Process

Baird organized his fourteen students into six design teams and scheduled the first five weeks of the semester term around analysis of Habitat's standard approach to design and construction, research regarding the various vinyl products typically utilized on Habitat homes (siding, windows, and so on.) Following this research phase, each team was charged with the task of designing a three-bedroom home that could be constructed for $55,000, the typical construction budget for homes built by HFHBR.

From the beginning of the studio, the issues associated with using vinyl-based products in the house "presented some pretty significant challenges" for Baird and his students. Habitat has long favored vinyl siding and windows for their affordability and (in the case of vinyl siding) the relative simplicity of installation—an important criteria in Habitat's "community volunteer" construction approach. However, Baird felt his students should know that the use of vinyl products has raised concern among many in the design industry, principally for the environmental issues arising from its manufacture and disposal. To make the issue even more complex, the vinyl industry is a major employer in the area around Baton Rouge, providing jobs for the families of several students in the studio.

Baird faced this challenge by exposing his students to both sides of "the vinyl debate," and allowed them as much latitude as possible in choosing the scope of vinyl products employed in the design. In the end, Baird estimates that the students reduced the amount of vinyl products utilized by almost half of what the affiliate would normally use in a Habitat home.

Another key issue that shaped the design process was the degree of access the students would have to the prospective homeowner during the design phase. "We really pushed hard to interview the family that we were designing for," reports Baird. This raised concerns within the affiliate leadership, who did not want to see the design deviate too broadly from their standards, or raise expectations among other prospective homeowners that they would have similar opportunities to customize their homes. According to Baird, "that was actually quite a negotiation," but he argued that the opportunity to respond to input from the client for the home was a crucial aspect of the learning experience for the students. Though concerns within the affiliate board lingered, Ruble agreed to allow the students to work directly with the homeowner, a single mother with three children, as they developed their design proposals.

At the conclusion of the five-week design stage the students, presented their designs to a panel of judges made up of architects invited by LSU, representatives from the Vinyl Institute, Ann Ruble and local architect Mark Montgomery, a long-time Habitat volunteer who had been designated "house leader," or project manager, by the affiliate. The judges selected two winning schemes, and suggested Baird and his students construct a house that blended the two designs.

The key design features of the hybrid design developed in response to the judges' request included a main entrance positioned on the southwest side of the plan that would be accessed via a fenced courtyard and shaded by a large existing tree on the site. The three exterior walls encompassing the courtyard were to be sheathed inside and out with a translucent polycarbonate material (Polygal™) that would admit natural light during the day and allow the interior light to illuminate the courtyard at night. The students' design for the interior spaces of the home featured stained concrete floors, lofted ceilings that mirrored the slope of the roof, and a custom "light shelf" above the kitchen area intended to define this area in the otherwise open plan encompassing the entrance area, the kitchen, and the living and dining spaces.

Baird and his students devoted the next five weeks of the semester to developing the hybrid design, completing construction drawings, applying for building permits, and soliciting in-kind material donations for the project. The students planned to construct a custom-designed lighting element for the kitchen ceiling using special fabrication equipment (including a CNC router) accessible to them on campus.

Construction Process

As the final month of the term approached, the students prepared to move on site to begin construction of the home. About this same time, Ann Ruble left her position as executive director of HFHBR. In Baird's view, this was a critical point in the project. Ruble had been the prime liaison between the affiliate and Baird's students, and her departure revealed that the HFHBR board was not as supportive of the design direction of the project as he heretofore thought.

The first indication of communication problems between the design team and the affiliate occurred when the students began preparing to move on site for the construction phase of the project. To their dismay, they discovered that the existing tree that was to have shaded the courtyard from the hot southwestern sun had been removed by the affiliate in the site-clearing process. As explained to

Baird, no one had indicated the role of the tree in the design strategy to the clearing crew, and they saw the tree as a risk to the house (due to the hurricane exposure of Baton Rouge) and a maintenance burden for the homeowner (trimming branches and raking leaves). Under pressure to complete the project before the end of the semester, the affiliate and the design team made the fateful decision to proceed with the proposed house orientation, despite the loss of shade from the tree.

As the construction progressed over the following month, Mark Montgomery moved into the role of prime affiliate contact for the students and helped them work through a number of construction details as the project progressed. For Montgomery, working with the students was a "great experience," but he reported frustrations of his own regarding communications with the design team. Despite his reservations regarding the durability of some of the construction details, such as the exposed framing at the roof eaves and the metal roof, Montgomery felt he "could not make any headway" with Baird and the students.

Despite these hurdles, Baird and his students saw the project through to completion by the end of April and the house dedication occurred in mid-May. The students worked on site during the weekdays and were joined by community volunteers and the homeowners on Saturdays.

Lessons Learned

Baird and Montgomery both agreed that the experience of both designing and building the VPH House was a great experience for the students. Based on entries in the journals Baird had the students maintain throughout the project, it was clear that "this was a life-changing thing for them," he noted. In interviews with media at the house dedication the students made it clear that they viewed the VPH House project as a special learning opportunity and that they wanted their efforts to be felt by the homeowner and her family: "Hopefully the design works to its fullest advantage, and the family enjoys the house that's been built. We want them to be excited about their home."[1]

In the eyes of Lynn Clark, who replaced Ann Ruble as director of the affiliate, the project was a "great partnership" between the affiliate, LSU, and the Vinyl Institute. However, in her view, "the design was outside the boundaries of what the affiliate board was comfortable with." Clark believes the affiliate would have been happier with a design that was "more in keeping with the look of the neighborhood" and one that reflected more input from the affiliate during the design phase. Montgomery echoes Clark's view, noting that the lack of involvement by more representatives from the affiliate (other than Ruble) was "a bit of a mistake."

The resolution of post-occupancy issues with the translucent polycarbonate sheathing around the courtyard walls came to symbolize the disconnect that developed between the design team and the affiliate board after Ruble's departure.

Within six months of occupancy, the new homeowner began expressing concerns that the house was too warm, regardless of the settings on the air-conditioning equipment. The affiliate attributed the problem to the unshaded polycarbonate around the courtyard, and Baird proposed that LSU should study the issue more closely to determine whether this was true. "We talked to the HVAC people and they said the air conditioning equipment should be sized and calibrated to cool that space adequately regardless of the sun exposure on the Polygal," notes Baird, adding, " we are not above admitting that maybe we have made an error, if in fact that's the case. We wanted to collect some data and analyze it. If we learn from it then we learn from it."

The affiliate did not believe this analysis was needed, and soon replaced the Polygal sections with conventional wall construction. Though Clark reports that this "solved the problem" with the warm interiors, Baird remains convinced that there may have been other solutions to the problem. "They [HFHBR] had made up their minds to switch the Polygal out regardless. To me that was really evident after Ann left—the Polygal was going to go."

Ruble's departure also marked a shift in the dialogue between the design team and the affiliate regarding the project cost. Clark reported that the VPH House "cost a good bit more than our typical house." According to Baird, his students had been aiming at a construction cost of approximately $55,000 with the understanding that they could add features that exceeded that budget only if they secured donations or extra funding (as was the case with the Polygal). Baird reports that Ruble and the students were in close communication regarding the cost estimate up to the point of her departure: "we had run some extensive numbers and our budget seemed to be in line with their 55,000–60,000 dollar target." However, Baird reports that, once construction began, "the numbers went underground and then they popped out and said we were up to 70–80 grand or something like that. I was kind of bewildered by it."

In Baird's view, the key challenges faced in the collaboration extend from differences in expectations regarding the goals of the project. The LSU team saw their involvement as an opportunity to "push the limits and to do something interesting and exciting," and believed that Ruble shared this goal. "She [Ruble] was interested in that, getting something different," said Baird.

Clark's post-mortem on the experience illustrates that the affiliate board did not see the goals of the partnership in the same light, noting that, "before we could become involved in [a collaboration like] this again, we would have to do a better job of communicating our criteria."

site plan

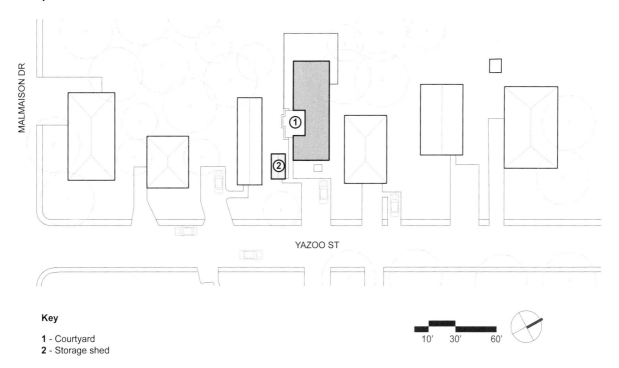

Key

1 - Courtyard
2 - Storage shed

10'   30'   60'

aerial view of house and courtyard

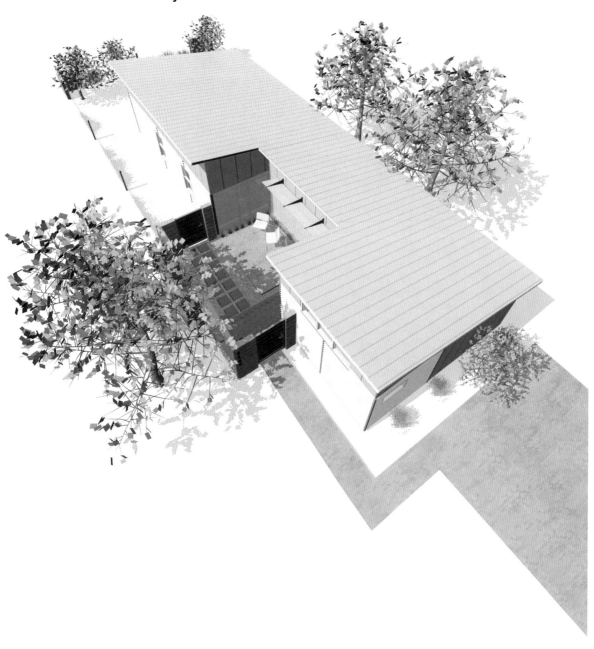

view of entry courtyard

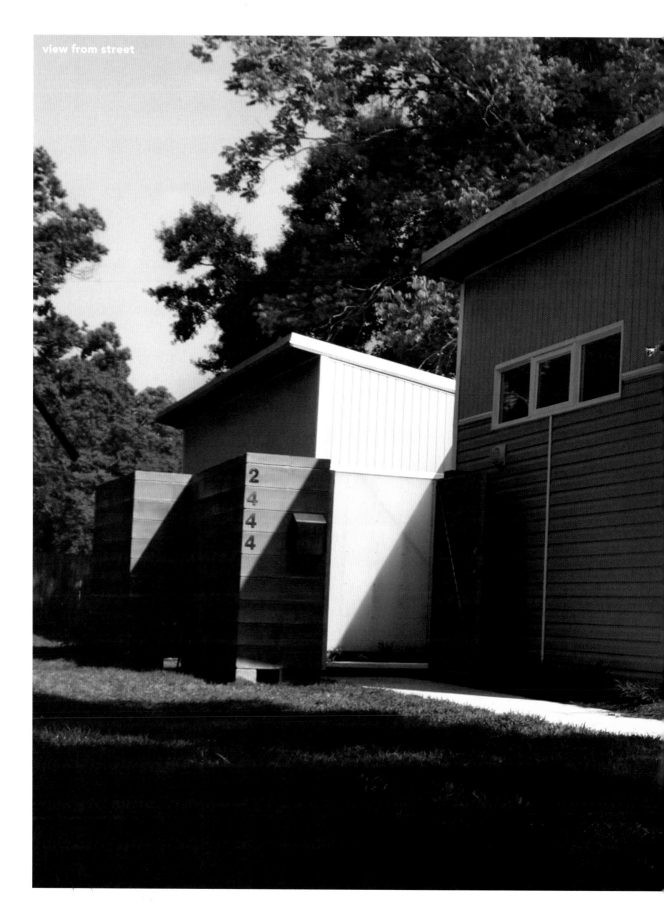

courtyard view

floor plan

Key

1 - Living
2 - Dining
3 - Kitchen
4 - Bath
5 - Bedroom
6 - Courtyard

1' 5' 10' 20'

view of kitchen and custom lighting fixture

interior view of Polygal walls

view of courtyard at night

Chapter 4

DESIGNhabitat 3

Atmore, Alabama

Auburn University, the Alabama Association of Habitat Affiliates, and Habitat for Humanity®
Escambia County (AL)

Key Partnerships

Justin Miller, Auburn University School of Architecture (AU)

Andy Bell, sustainable building specialist, Alabama Association of Habitat Affiliates (AAHA)

Rusty Miller, building coordinator and building committee chairperson,

      Habitat for Humanity Escambia County (HFHEC) (DESIGNhabitat 3.0)

      Habitat for Humanity Hale County (DESIGNhabitat 3.1)

Pamela Dorr, executive director, Habitat for Humanity Hale County (HFHHC)

Program Summary

DESIGNhabitat 3.0 home

2-bedroom, 1-bath, single-family detached home

930 square feet

DESIGNhabitat 3.1 home

2-bedroom, 1-bath, single-family detached home

970 square feet

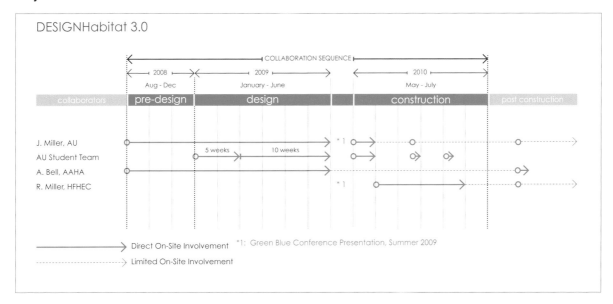

Catalysts for Collaboration

As profiled in Chapter 1, Auburn University's School of Architecture (AU) and the Alabama Association of Habitat for Humanity Affiliates (AAHA) have used the DESIGNhabitat program to develop innovative design strategies and prototypes for Habitat homes throughout Alabama. Through 2008, this partnership, which involves homeowners, student researchers, designers and constructors, local affiliates, state HFH coordinators, and School of Architecture faculty, has resulted in two rounds of successful collaboration.

In 2008 Habitat for Humanity International and the Home Depot Foundation initiated "Partners in Sustainable Building," a pilot program designed to increase green building practices among "thirty Habitat affiliates across a variety of climates in rural and urban areas throughout the United States" by providing financial and technical assistance to affiliates through grants to HFH state support organizations.[1] Based in part on the track record of success in its partnership with Auburn, AAHA was one of four state support organizations included in the first round of Partners in Sustainable Building grant awards.

In November of 2008, Andy Bell, AAHA's sustainable building specialist, and Justin Miller, a faculty member in AU's School of Architecture, began a series of discussions regarding the possibility of a third round of the DESIGNhabitat program, specifically a studio that would result in a set of Energy Star DESIGNhabitat house plans that Bell could make available to HFH affiliates across the state.

While these discussions were underway, the Gadsden–Etowah County Habitat affiliate contacted Bell regarding their interest in incorporating Energy Star certification in a home they were planning to build in the coming year. Bell asked Miller to begin the DESIGNhabitat 3 studio with a study aimed at helping HFH Gadsden–Etowah County, and Miller agreed.[2]

Design Process

In the spring semester of 2009, Miller organized a group of fifteen third- and fourth-year undergraduate architecture students to begin three phases of design research, beginning with the redesign of the DESIGNhabitat 1 house. As Miller recalls, "with little time for the students to conduct research, the redesign of the first DESIGNhabitat house provided the students with an intense introduction to the design strategies the previous classes had utilized."

The first phase of design research allowed the students to understand Habitat's design guidelines and introduced the challenge of designing affordable housing. Organized into teams of three, the students developed modified versions of the DESIGNhabitat 1 house and presented the designs to Steve Sharfenberg, executive director of HFH Gadsden–Etowah, the prospective homeowners, and Bell in early February. The discussions with the homeowner and Sharfenberg, as Miller recalls, "provided valuable feedback for all of us. We learned a lot from the affiliate as well as from the homeowner."

Following the presentation to the Gadsden–Etowah affiliate, the students began a focused two-week-long research phase that "sought to understand the requirements of Energy Star certification as well as to assess other green building rating programs," recalls Miller. Additionally the students sought to re-visit the question raised in the DESIGNhabitat 2 homes: what is the appropriate mix of prefabrication and on-site construction in Habitat homes?

Primed by the research phase, the student teams began developing design proposals for the DESIGNhabitat 3 prototypes. Bell was a frequent visitor to the studio as the students' designs took shape, giving workshops on the Home Energy Rating System (HERS) utilized in the Energy Star Homes program and providing feedback to the students on their designs. As Miller notes, Bell was also "instrumental in helping the studio evaluate the viability of energy performance options with respect to the ability of Habitat's volunteer builders to meet the performance level targeted."

Bell and Miller also worked with the students to help them understand the parameters of the "Partners in Sustainable Building" pilot program. According to Miller, the criteria of this program were fairly straightforward: affiliates could receive a direct cash subsidy ($3000) if they built a home that met Energy Star requirements and up to $5000 if the affiliate had their home certified under a national or regional certification standard (such as Alabama EnergyKey, EarthCraft, or LEED® for Homes).

Miller established two primary goals for the students to meet in their prototype designs: "they were asked to identify passive and active energy conservations strategies that would allow the designs to achieve Energy Star certification (or better), as well as to develop a strategy for varying the level of prefabrication the design might employ," said Miller. After working through a "parent" version of their homes based on a three-bedroom scheme, the teams were also asked to quickly test whether or not that scheme could logically morph into a two-bedroom or four-bedroom house. After verifying the plausibility of that approach, they were tasked with developing both a cost estimate and energy performance estimate. As Miller notes, "this was a bit ambitious."

Bell met with the teams throughout the course of the semester in a series of "analysis charrettes" to consult on energy performance by using REM/RATE™ (energy-modeling software) to assist in determining HERS Index numbers for all of the teams. A HERS Index is a score that is determined by using a computer program (REM/RATE) to assess a design with respect to its specific location. The HERS Index is measured on a scale ranging from 0 to 150+, with 100 representing a design that conforms to the 2009 International Energy Conservation Code (IECC) standards, while a lower number represents performance better than code. Bell analyzed each team's design utilizing the REM/RATE software and gave each a projected HERS score.

The initial HERS score provided a sobering "reality check" for the students, notes Miller. "We were all over the board at the initial testing with Andy, from the 50s to the 120s," Miller recalled. Bell and Miller helped each team understand the specific aspects of their schemes that were having the most detrimental impact on their HERS score. After a second round of design studies, and analysis by Bell, all the schemes met or exceeded Energy Star certification requirements (85 HERS Index).

At the conclusion of the studio the students were invited to present their prototype designs at the AAHA Annual Conference. The student teams presented material that described the design objectives, cost estimates, and projected HERS scores for each prototype along with a viable path to achieving certification by one of the national or regional certification programs.

As a component of its Partners in Sustainability grant, AAHA organized a green building conference (the Green and Blue Conference) early in the spring of 2010, and asked Miller to present the results of the DESIGNhabitat 3 program at the conference. As Bell recalls, Rusty Miller, building coordinator and building committee chairperson for Habitat for Humanity Escambia County (HFHEC), was gearing up to build a house under the Partners in Sustainable Building program. Bell encouraged him to attend the conference, where he saw Miller's presentation. Rusty Miller approached Justin Miller about tailoring one of the DESIGNhabitat 3 prototypes for HFHEC.

Construction Process

Over the course of the spring of 2010, Justin Miller and Rusty Miller continued to discuss the possibility of HFHEC building one of the DESIGNhabitat 3 prototype designs on a site in Atmore, Alabama. This would be the first home constructed by HFHEC in Atmore and there was some concern over the number of volunteers that would make the trip to the site. As Rusty discussed the project, it became clear that the opportunity to build on the Atmore site would present both the opportunity to test the energy conservation strategies incorporated in the students' work, and the chance to test the students' suggestion that the design was well-suited to construction via prefabricated components as a way of building with a small team of on-site volunteers.

Justin Miller asked Mark Porth and Daniel Beeker, two of the students from the DESIGNhabitat 3 studio who had designed the selected prototype, to review the team's two-bedroom prototype design and revise the design drawings to respond to the affiliate's site and their prefabrication approach.

The site identified for the house had a substantial front-to-back down slope. As rotating the house was not feasible due to the narrow lot width, the home would need to have a taller-than-average foundation, which would have increased the cost of the home substantially. As Justin notes, "Beeker and Porth saw this as an opportunity to test the practicality of a pier foundation," which they hoped would reduce the cost substantially compared with a block foundation wall.

Justin Miller worked with Beeker and Porth to develop a set of construction drawings along with a description of the design features critical to the energy performance goals (types of assemblies, materials, and insulation values, and so on), which Rusty (a skilled builder with his own construction firm) used for construction. As Justin Miller notes, "we were a little nervous about handing the project off to someone else to build. A large part of the success of the prior DESIGNhabitat collaborations was a result of the involvement of the design team in both the design and construction phases." After a series of discussions to clarify assembly details and materials, Rusty was ready to organize his crew of HFHEC volunteers.

Construction of the house began in May of 2010. According to Rusty the layout of the pier foundation was relatively easy, and he was surprised by "how little concrete the system actually required." In the following weeks the affiliate constructed the sub-floor and floor and was ready to begin the wall framing. Rusty had taken the design team's suggestion to test the use of prefabricated wall panels and roof trusses. According to Rusty, "the panels and trusses arrived on site and were installed over the course of a weekend." As Miller recounts, the volunteers who returned the next week, not expecting to see a house on the site, "found the house almost completely framed."

The affiliate was very attentive to achieving the design team's intended insulation levels for the house. The wall panels (pre-framed with 2 × 6 studs) provided additional cavity space for cellulose insulation, which was paired with a half-inch layer of rigid insulation on the exterior of the assembly. Miller also installed the radiant barrier roof sheathing recommended by the DESIGNhabitat design team.

Team member Daniel Beeker traveled to the site several times over the course of the construction process to work alongside the homeowners and the HFHEC volunteers. The completed home was dedicated in July of 2010.

In September, Justin Miller, Andy Bell, and Mark Porth met Rusty Miller at the house to test the house's air tightness and duct leakage to determine the actual HERS Index score for the house. Though testing indicated that the air leakage numbers were a little higher than expected the big revelation had to do with the mechanical system. The house's mechanical system, comprised of an indoor and outdoor unit, did not have matching serial numbers. According to Bell this might not have a major impact on the performance of the system; however, it did mean that the house would not achieve Energy Star certification until the discrepancy could be resolved.

Alabama Habitat affiliates have continued to build homes from the DESIGNhabitat 3 portfolio. HFH Hale County completed a DESIGNhabitat 3.1 home in 2011, and HFH Escambia County completed another home (their second) in 2012. Of the five prototype designs developed in 2009, three have been constructed to date. As with the first home, Miller has provided assistance and support to the affiliates to help them construct the home consistent with the design and performance goals of the DESIGNhabitat program.

Lesson Learned

From Miller's perspective, the DESIGNhabitat 3 project offered a number of lessons. Among those lessons is the need to "go slowly and really get to know your partners," said Miller. Miller notes that "the complexity of something seemingly as straight-forward as a 'simple decent home' is really challenging for the students, and faculty." Seeing the energy-use consequences of their design proposals, the students were confronted with the fact that the design decisions they make have a significant impact upon the lives of their clients. Low-income families in the state and region spend approximately 33 percent of their income on utilities and any decrease (or increase) in utility costs has a significant impact on homeowners. Miller notes that the students came to see "that the implications of those decisions extend beyond spatial/aesthetic considerations and into the foundations of the homeowner family's economic security."

For both Bell and Justin Miller, an additional success of the studio was the opportunity for the students to experience the impact of performance testing *during* the design process. Having Bell as the studio's "energy consultant" both allowed the students the experience of engaging a specialist consultant in the design studio (something that will be central to their experience in practice), and it allowed the students to respond to the consultant's feedback and incorporate that feedback into the design process. For Miller, in-process building performance evaluations forced the students to revise their designs until they met the target performance objective. As Miller notes "the first round of HERS Index scores were instrumental in focusing the students' energies."

Miller also saw the pressure to meet the design and construction goals of the studio push students to begin to "think holistically about a design proposal and draw upon material (such as coursework in mechanical systems and building construction) that had been covered in prior semesters of their education."

From the affiliate's perspective the collaboration was a success, even with the difficulty surrounding the still unresolved Energy Star certification. Rusty Miller notes that many of the new systems and construction approaches used in the DESIGNhabitat 3 house, including the use of the pier foundation system and panelized walls, are "construction approaches we might try again."

Justin Miller notes the transition from building the houses with the student design team to preparing documents for affiliates to build from was a learning experience in its own right. "The construction phase was a bit of a challenge for us. Handing off the design was a new approach, and we really needed to be more involved in the construction process," observed Miller. Other affiliates are lining up to build homes in the DESIGNhabitat 3 portfolio in the coming year and, according to Miller, the experience of constructing the first house with HFHEC "makes clear the necessity to tighten up communication through the entire process."

FRONT PERSPECTIVE | A

BACK PERSPECTIVE | B

setting prefabricated wall panels

DESIGNhabitat 3.0 floor plan

Key

1 - Living
2 - Dining
3 - Kitchen
4 - Bath
5 - Bedroom
6 - Porch

1'   5'   10'   20'

prototype design concepts and strategies

CONCEPTS AND STRATEGIES
site diagram + vegetation

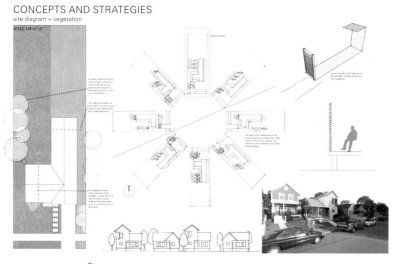

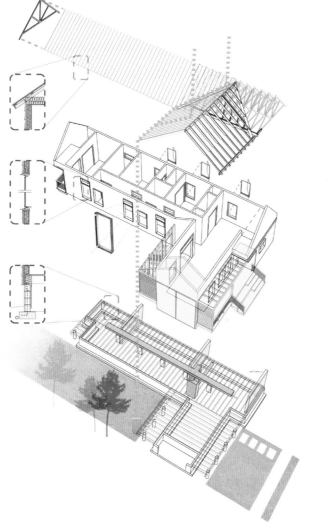

DESIGNhabitat 3.0 home dedication

DESIGNhabitat 3.1 floor plan

Key

1 - Living
2 - Dining
3 - Kitchen
4 - Bath
5 - Bedroom
6 - Porch

1'   5'   10'   20'

view from rear yard

Chapter 5

habiTECH09

Ruston, Louisiana

Louisiana Tech University and Habitat for Humanity® North Central Louisiana

Key Partnerships

Kevin Stevens, Louisiana Tech University School of Architecture (LTUSA)

Allen Tuten, board of directors (former executive director), Habitat for Humanity North Central Louisiana (HFHNCL)

Chip Henderson, Contects: Consultants and Architects

Program Summary

3-bedroom, 1.5-bath single-family detached home

1,150 square feet

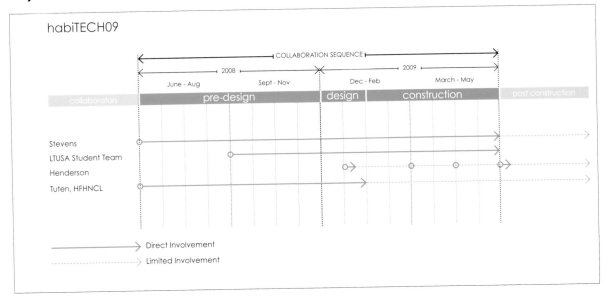

Catalysts for Collaboration

habiTECH is an initiative within Louisiana Tech University's School of Architecture that engages fifth-year architecture students in a research-based, design/build experience involving active collaboration with the local Habitat affiliate, Habitat for Humanity North Central Louisiana (HFHNCL), as well as prospective Habitat homeowners.

The initiative, now directed by professor Kevin Stevens, began in 2004 when Karl Puljak (then director of the School of Architecture's design/build program) and members of the HFHNCL board of directors began discussing the possibility of working together to have LTUSA students design and build a Habitat home.

For LTUSA, a complete single-family home was a big jump in scale from previous work that had been undertaken by the design/build program, both in scale and in the resources needed to support the effort. Puljak and HFHNCL secured a $20,000 grant from the Weyerhaeuser Corporation that provided financial support to the design effort and helped support construction of the first "habiTECH" house, completed in 2006.

The success of the initial habiTECH home project provided the impetus for renewed rounds of collaboration, leading to the construction of five habiTECH houses through 2011 (a sixth is currently in progress). Each successive house has incorporated innovative design strategies along with new/novel materials, "technologies that are outside of the mainstream local building industry," noted Stevens.

In each round of collaboration the students were presented a consistent set of goals that stress the importance of designing and building houses that are "as environmentally sound as possible and respectful of Habitat's standards," according to Stevens. In addition to these basic goals the students were asked to engage in direct dialogue with the partner family and work with them throughout the design process. Lastly – and most critically for Stevens – "the students in the studio had to collectively come up with a mission statement, if you will, that identified a precise element, system, or set of ideas that they, as a class, were interested in pursuing."

Over the course of the summer of 2008 Stevens met with HFHNCL's staff and directors to discuss the outcome of the recently completed habiTECH08 house. Stevens described the meetings as "a series of casual conversations" about the project designed to "fine tune and work on that relationship over the course of the following project." The meetings also provided the opportunity to discuss the upcoming year's house, set a "top end budget," and to try to identify potential sites. With approval from the HFHNCL board, Stevens and Allen Tuten (then executive director of HFHNCL) began planning for the fall quarter.

Design Process

In the fall of 2008 a group of nine undergraduate architecture students began the habiTECH09 project via a design research methods seminar, led by Stevens, which was designed to immerse the students in the project and to develop the specific goals that would shape the subsequent design effort.[1] Over the following two academic terms (winter and spring), the students would design and build the house as part of their final design studio sequence.

At the beginning of the design research methods seminar the students engaged in a series of meetings with the affiliate in an effort, says Stevens, to start "a long conversation introducing the players." Stevens organized the initial meetings to allow the students to interview the affiliate and familiarize themselves with the framework of issues that would shape the design, including the affiliate's design and construction standards, their organizational structure, and the affiliate's budget and goals for the project.

Following the initial meetings with the affiliate, the students were engaged in the affiliate's family selection process. As Tuten described the process, once the homeowner was selected, "the students were involved in a series of conversations with the homeowner family to determine family size and what their particular needs might be, what their priority wish list might be." For Stevens this was a critical and valuable experience for the students, as they were able to "go with Habitat representatives to interview the families in their homes and see the living conditions they were dealing with and the reality of that situation."

After determining HFHNCL's goals and those specific to the homeowner, Stevens asked the students to develop the "mission statement" that identified "the precise element, system, or set of ideas that they as a class would be interested in pursuing." As Stevens recounts, the students "wanted to investigate LEED® as a system for project delivery and find out exactly what that means for an affordable residence." By the conclusion of the fall term, the students had compiled their research into a report that incorporated their research, their understanding of HFHNCL's goals, and a program for the house that called for three bedrooms and one full-, and one half-bath. The students also set a goal of LEED for Homes Silver certification for the project, which would be a first for the habiTECH program and for HFHNCL.

At the beginning of the winter term the students were split into two teams to develop design proposals for the habiTECH09 house, and their initial schemes presented some areas of concern for Stevens. As he recalls, "when students first presented the study models, they were pretty aggressive … the overall form of the house was an issue and the [proposed] use of metal siding was also something of a hot-button issue."

The students were quick to respond to the critique provided by Stevens, and worked to support their design proposals with more evidence that the proposals would result in improved building performance. "They began to do things like solar studies showing how the roof form was shading the interior of the house, how daylighting was being introduced from the north through the clerestory lighting above the kitchen area." The students were ultimately able to justify their material choices "with a lot of data why this material was a great decision," noted Stevens.

Following a series of intensive design sessions, or "charrettes," with numerous LTUSA faculty members, the designs were presented to the homeowner, HFHNCL representatives, and LTUSA faculty for selection of the final scheme to advance to construction by the studio. The scheme selected by the jury organizes the bedroom spaces and bathrooms into a rectangular volume, while the public area of the house (living room, kitchen, and dining room) opens to a street-facing front porch and a large back porch (a specific request of the partner family).

The orientation of the site selected for the home required the long sides of the house to face east and west, which presented problems in terms of glazing area and concerns of overheating. In an effort to resolve the less-than-ideal site orientation, the selected scheme minimized east and west windows and introduced light into the interior through clerestory windows that brought north light into the open kitchen and living area.

Toward the middle of November the final design was presented to the full HFHNCL board and the homeowner. With their approval secured, the students worked on completing construction drawings, securing permits, estimating costs, and (in collaboration with the LEED provider) evaluating the LEED credits that were achievable on the project. With advice and assistance from LEED consultant Chip Henderson, the students assessed the opportunities for LEED credits and decided to utilize a series of construction strategies new to HFHNCL, including Optimum Value Engineered (OVE) framing (2 × 6 wood framing @ 24" on center) for the wall construction and Structural Insulated Panel System (SIPS) for the roof construction. The roof is comprised of two distinct corrugated metal roof forms, which collect and divert rain to a rain barrel for use in site irrigation.

Construction Process

In mid-January the student team began construction of the home, which continued over the next four months. As Tuten recalls, "the students were out there five to six days week and seven days a week at the end of construction." HFHNCL volunteers came out on Saturdays to lend a hand.

The process set up by Stevens and HFHNCL held the students responsible for managing the budget and for staying within the budget approved by the HFHNCL board. The students were given the authority to search out and purchase materials and invoices were brought to HFHNCL on a monthly basis for payment. Throughout the construction process the students made monthly presentations to the affiliate's board of directors regarding cost and schedule. The students were able to acquire additional donations and grants for the home that supported the LEED certification. From Tuten's perspective this process worked pretty well: "the out-of-pocket costs for the chapter were about the same as one of our pretty vanilla plans."

The student team completed construction of the habiTECH09 house (on budget and on target for LEED for Homes certification) on the 19th of May, one day before the students' graduation. After attending an early-morning home dedication the students proceeded back to campus for their commencement ceremony.

After construction was completed the house was tested by energy rater Chip Henderson to see if the completed home would meet the standards the students had hoped to achieve. The tests established that the house achieved a score of 67 on the HERS Index. An 85 is required for Energy Star certification, and the project qualified for the targeted LEED Silver certification – the first house in Northern Louisiana to achieve LEED for Homes certification.

Lessons Learned

In Tuten's view, the collaborations with LTUSA have helped the affiliate on several fronts. On a basic level, the partnership has helped HFHNCL double their annual home construction capacity (typically the affiliate builds one house per year). At the same time the partnership has introduced the affiliate to innovative approaches to construction that would not have been pursued without the habiTECH collaborations. Though "there has been some concern about specific material choices," notes Tuten, several of the habiTECH homes have introduced valuable issues to HFHNCL and have influenced their decisions regarding use of more durable materials and more volunteer-builder-friendly assemblies. The students have also introduced the affiliate to the advantages of prefabricated roof trusses. "It's not a whole lot more expensive but certainly time and labor saving," noted Tuten. "We will probably do that more in the future than we have in the past."

Though the affiliate is quite active in the planning and design phases of the project, both Tuten and Stevens believe the transfer of lessons (between the habiTECH projects and the affiliate) regarding both design and construction approaches was complicated by the limited involvement of the affiliate on the building site. From Stevens's perspective it was important for the students to understand the client's needs – and that included working with HFHNCL both in the studio and in the field. Stevens was hopeful that future habiTECH projects will address this shortcoming.

Both Stevens and Tuten pointed to the value of the students' interactions with the partner family in the development of the houses. From Stevens's perspective, the opportunity to work with the client allowed the students to consider the needs of the family, to address the concerns of the children, and to "carve out a little space for them" in the design. Impressed with the quality and thoughtfulness of the students' work, Tuten notes, "they have done a lot toward individualizing the designs for the needs of family members. Whereas we may have been very vanilla in that regard, the students have been more in tune with the individual needs of the family. For example, families often have a couple of children and the students designs' include a place to study in their bedroom or a common study area with built-in desks provided."

Although the habiTECH09 house achieved LEED Silver certification, both Stevens and Tuten are unsure that they will pursue it in the future. From Stevens's perspective, the energy conservation strategies employed to achieve the certification "did take hold with the affiliate." However, "the value of the LEED certification [itself] did not seem clear."

According to Tuten, working with LTUSA has moved the affiliate toward employing more energy conservation measures in the homes they build and to thinking about sustainability in broader terms. As Tuten notes, "the students tried to take into consideration future maintenance, utility costs and usage, placement of windows to conserve energy and bring in natural light, and green space around the houses. They have been very conscientious [about designing] for the future."

The experience of collaborating over a sustained length of time has also helped LTUSA and the affiliate understand and support each other's goals for the partnership. As Stevens noted, once students are involved "not only is there the important factor of delivering housing, but there also has to be opportunities for the students to investigate and pursue [new ideas] as part of their education."

For both Stevens and Tuten, the success of the collaboration also rested on open lines of communication and trust built up over four years of collaboration, and on the continuity of affiliate leadership at HFHNCL since the first house in 2006. Though Tuten has retired from his position as executive director of the affiliate, he remains on the board and serves as liaison to Stevens and the habiTECH student teams.

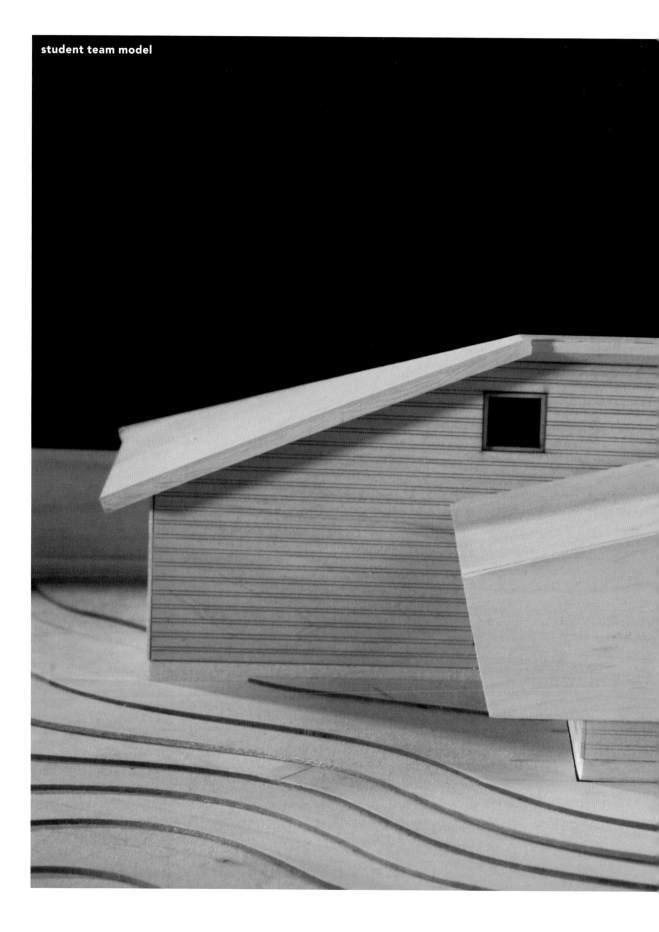

view of entry from street

floor plan

Key

1 - Living
2 - Dining
3 - Kitchen
4 - Half Bath
5 - Bath
6 - Bedroom
7 - Porch

1'   5'   10'   20'

view toward kitchen area and entry

view to back porch from kitchen/living area

ecoMOD4

Charlottesville, Virginia

University of Virginia and Habitat for Humanity® Greater Charlottesville (VA)

Key Partnerships

John Quale, University of Virginia School of Architecture (UVASA)

Paxton Marshall, University of Virginia School of Engineering and Applied Sciences

Dan Rosensweig, executive director, Habitat for Humanity Greater Charlottesville (HFHC)

Audrey Storm, director of construction services, Habitat for Humanity Greater Charlottesville

Program Summary

2-bedroom, 1.5-bath, single-family detached home

1,130 square feet

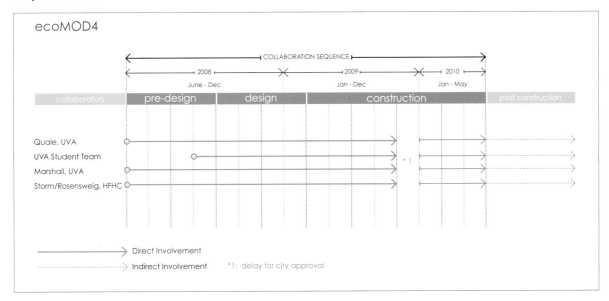

Catalysts for Collaboration

ecoMOD is an award-winning initiative within the School of Architecture at the University of Virginia devoted to exploring how advanced construction techniques and technologies can be used to produce affordable homes that consume fewer resources to build and operate.[1] One of the primary advanced construction techniques at the center of the ecoMOD program is modular prefabrication.

Led by professor John Quale, the ecoMOD program engages architecture and engineering students in what Quale describes as a "design/build/evaluate" cycle of design-based research that allows the students to gain hands-on experience of design and construction, along with the experience of collaborating with non-profit housing organizations. To date, the program has produced five homes, including two homes for Habitat affiliates. Each ecoMOD home is constructed by Quale's students in a former airplane hangar in large modules or panels, and trucked to its construction site for on-site assembly.

The first collaboration between UVASA and Habitat (ecoMOD2) was a panelized home completed in 2006 for a family displaced by Hurricane Katrina.[2] The home was designed and fabricated in Charlottesville by Quale and his students, and erected in Gulfport, Mississippi. HFHC was the sponsoring affiliate for this house and several members of the affiliate board were very involved in this project. The experience of this first partnership was positive for both groups: "ecoMOD2 gave us the opportunity to know them (HFHC), and to understand their point of view ... and they got excited about working with the students," observed Quale. The trust developed between UVASA and HFHC on ecoMOD2 left both groups interested in finding another opportunity to collaborate.

Quale and his students were committed to a project with another non-profit housing group in 2007 (ecoMOD3), but discussions between Quale and Audrey Storm, HFHC's director of construction services, set the stage for the two groups to work together in 2008.

Several objectives came to shape the second round of the ecoMOD/ HFHC partnership. With eight EarthCraft Certified homes completed prior to this project, the HFHC had already established a commitment to building more sustainable homes. According to Storm, the affiliate saw LEED® certification as an opportunity to access additional grant funding for future projects, and she noted, "we were eager to understand what building to the LEED standards would be getting us in to." According to Dan Rosensweig, HFHC Executive Director, the opportunity to partner with UVASA would allow the affiliate to "push the envelope," test out new ways to integrate green technologies into their homes, and "find out whether sustainable was attainable" in the framework of Habitat's affordable-housing development model. The project site (donated by the City of Charlottesville) also presented some significant challenges regarding limited site utility infrastructure and a narrow lot width. According to Quale, "this made for a perfect site to do something different."

Quale and the leadership of HFHC worked through the summer of 2008 to reach agreements on the objectives of the project, the project process and schedule, the division of responsibility between UVASA and the affiliate for con-struction of the project, and how the project would be funded. HFHC agreed to provide $60,000 toward the construction and Quale agreed to secure an additional $60,000 to cover the cost of advanced technologies and construction methods that would be incorporated into the project. The responsibilities of each party and other details of their agreement were outlined in a Memorandum of Understanding (MOU) signed by both groups.

Design Process

Quale and his students began work in September of 2008 with the beginning of the fall term. The interdisciplinary team was comprised of nineteen undergraduate and graduate architecture students, along with twenty-one engineering students working under the direction of professor Paxton Marshall from the School of Engineering and Applied Sciences at the University of Virginia. As the architecture students investigated alternative design and construction approaches; the engineering students studied stormwater solutions, structural design options, and mechanical systems alternatives.

Over the course of the fall, the students worked in teams to develop design ideas for key components of the project. Pushed forward via two intensive design sessions, made up of students from all the disciplines involved in the project along with Rosensweig and Audrey Storm, the design proposals gradually coalesced into a three-bedroom prototype home design.

The prospective homeowner was identified by the affiliate in October, prompting a revision of the program from three to two bedrooms and a few other refinements to the program of required spaces to accommodate the homeowner's needs. As the range of design alternatives narrowed, key design goals began to emerge, including an emphasis on natural light within the house and views out into the site—employed to make the small house "feel bigger," according to Quale. By the end of the term, the students put forward a final design option, which was approved by HFHC.

As the spring semester began, Quale began to organize his students into teams (each led by a student serving as project/construction manager) focused on a specific aspect of the project, ranging from design refinement and systems engineering to planning out the prefabricated construction process and materials procurement. "We were fortunate to have some mature students with construction experience involved in the studio and they played key leadership roles," reports Quale.

Concurrent with the refinement of the design, Quale and the student construction managers met frequently with Storm and Rosensweig to talk about budgeting for the evolving design and to carefully plan the construction and material procurement process. "We did not want [this project] to make extra work for the affiliate," noted Quale, "so we figured out a way to link our budget to their invoicing and bookkeeping systems. We set up a clear method for approving purchases for materials, and so on. This all developed over the course of a *lot* of meetings."

This emphasis on detailed planning of the construction, budgeting, and cost tracking arose from Quale's past experience working with non-profits, and it proved critical to managing the relationship with HFHC. In particular, notes Quale, "this approach built up [the affiliate's] confidence that the ecoMOD team could really keep to their budget."

Interactions with the HFHC's Building Committee, made up of experienced construction volunteers and local architects, also proved valuable for Quale's students. The detailed scrutiny and "Can you really do it that way?" questions from the committee "provided the voice of reality—exactly what they needed to hear," observed Quale.

The ecoMOD4 house, dubbed the "Thru House" by the students for its emphasis on cross-ventilation and abundant daylighting, was planned as two large modules, one encompassing all the spaces of the first level (the living area, dining area, and kitchen) and one for the second level, consisting of the two bedrooms and the bath. Though prior ecoMOD homes have utilized Structural Insulated Panel System (SIPS), steel framing, and other advanced wall systems, the ecoMOD4 house was "stick framed" to make it more consistent with Habitat's standard wood-framed construction approach. "We wanted to see how we could maximize the performance of the building envelope within the volunteer-based construction approaches Habitat could replicate," notes Quale, "and the students really embraced this challenge."

Construction Process

A grant from the local utility, Dominion Power, covered the cost of a photovoltaic panel system for the house and the incorporation of "smart meter" technology, allowing power usage to be measured for separate systems in the house. The addition of these technologies allowed the team to pursue a "net zero energy use" performance goal and a LEED Gold certification.

As the end of the spring term approached, Quale's team moved from the design studio to the hangar and began construction of the modules. Though some of the students had to end their involvement with the end of the term, most continued work on the project through the summer and fall, and new students joined the team for this phase of the work. Several students were so committed to the project, notes Quale, that they chose to work past their graduation from UVASA. Part of the funding secured by Quale provided living stipends for the summer work crew.

The UVASA students (joined by the future homeowners) worked through the summer and fall to complete the modules at the hangar. In an adjustment to the initial MOU with HFHC, the students also took on the construction of the insulated concrete formwork (ICF) foundations for the home and other site development work when the affiliate found itself stretched too thin to handle these elements of the project as planned. Though this expansion of the students' scope of work was initially seen as a setback, in the end, according to Quale, "the challenge of regrouping and solving the problem was a significant contribution to the learning experience of the students."

The modules were set on the completed foundations in October and the final on-site construction elements were finished within a few weeks. Complications related to negotiations with the city over utility connections pushed the final completion and dedication of the home to May of 2010.[3]

Lessons Learned

From the beginning, HFHC saw this project as an opportunity to build on and expand their commitment to building "greener" homes, according to Rosensweig. Based on prior experience with the ecoMOD program, HFHC knew that Quale and his team could investigate design and construction options well beyond the normal reach of the affiliate, and they could provide an in-depth analysis of how well the innovative features of the project were working. "While our core model for projects will always be simple, decent, and affordable," notes Rosensweig, "we are willing to push the envelope with special projects like this one if it helps us advance our understanding of how to build better homes."

Rosensweig also noted that the ecoMOD team's efforts to "understand the [decision] drivers" of the affiliate, including their approach to project budgeting and the role of volunteer-builders in their process, were key factors in the project's success.

Quale also credits the emphasis on clear communications—especially regarding design expectations, budget, and a "working process." In Quale's view, the MOU crafted in the summer of 2008 to address these issues set the stage for the partnership with HFHC and "allowed everyone the confidence to aim high."

Based on the assessments of both Quale and Rosensweig the ecoMOD4 collaboration was very successful. From the HFHC side of the project, the ecoMOD4 house, along with the research and analysis developed by the students to produce it and measure its performance, has allowed the affiliate to refine its green building strategy and strengthened its commitment to lowering homeowners' energy costs. Though Rosensweig notes that the contemporary aesthetic of the house was "outside the mainstream" for many members of the HFHC board, the design of the home proved to be a "good fit" for the homeowner family who "are ecstatic about it," according to Rosensweig.

Storm and Rosensweig note that several of the solutions incorporated into the house have promise for migration into the affiliate's standard approach, including ICF foundations, switched electrical receptacles, and pervious concrete paving. Rosensweig also reports that the project has given HFHC confidence that the mandates of LEED certification translate to worthwhile benefits to their homeowner families. HFHC has subsequently completed two LEED-certified duplex homes via collaborations with local architects (including a second modular home) and has several ambitious green building initiatives in development.

From Quale's perspective, the challenge of working within the framework of HFHC while pushing to explore new ideas on the project provided a "powerful education experience based on real-world problems" for his students.

Both Quale and Rosensweig emphasize that the foundations of that success were the careful effort to align expectations of both parties at the beginning of the project, the agreement to frame the project as an opportunity to "aim high" and explore innovative design and construction approaches, and the emphasis on communication and coordination between Quale's team and the HFHC affiliate.

construction of module in UVA hanger

setting module

floor plan

Ground Floor

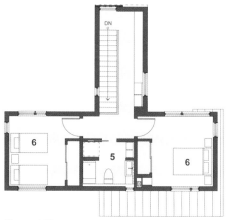

Second Floor

Key

1 - Living   4 - Half Bath   7 - Deck
2 - Dining   5 - Bath
3 - Kitchen   6 - Bedroom

1'   5'   10'   20'

GROUP

TWO

COLLABORATIONS WITH ARCHITECTS

Chapter 7

Project 1800

Philadelphia, Pennsylvania

Sally Harrison and Habitat for Humanity® North Philadelphia (PA)

Key Partnerships

Sally Harrison, architect and professor at Temple University Department of Architecture (TU)

Terry Jacobs, architect and partner with Jacobs Wyper Architects

John Collins, landscape architect and principal of the Delta Group

Orleans Homebuilders

Jon Musselman, construction manager, Habitat for Humanity North Philadelphia (HFHNP)*

* The affiliates in the Philadelphia area merged into a single affiliate in 2000 to become Habitat for Humanity Philadelphia. This project was undertaken by the North Philadelphia affiliate prior to the merger.

Program Summary

Seven 3-bedroom, 1-bath attached units

1,300 square feet

Seven 4-bedroom, 1.5-bath attached units

1,400 square feet

Four rehabilitated row house shells

Size varies

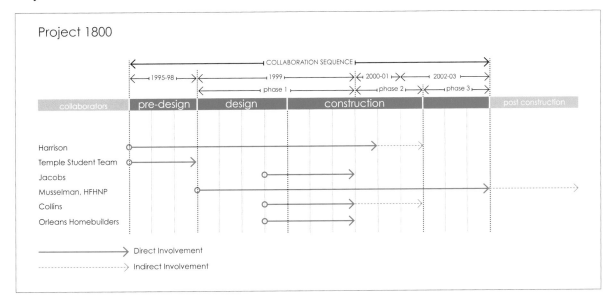

Catalysts for Collaboration

By the mid-1990s the neighborhoods around Temple University's North Philadelphia campus were in a serious decline, decimated by decades of suburban migration and poverty-related crime. Sally Harrison, an architect and member of the architecture faculty at Temple, began studying the neighborhoods of North Philadelphia and began to work with the community to re-create a viable plan for reinvestment in the area centered on affordable housing.

One of the key problems Harrison identified was what she viewed as well-intentioned, but misguided, effort to address the problem area with inappropriate design strategies. The city and a number of non-profit agencies (including Habitat) had been clearing derelict properties and supporting new housing construction, but their efforts to build suburban-style detached homes in the place of demolished row houses was, in Harrison's view, "creating houses, but not building neighborhoods."[1]

Through a gradual process of site acquisition aided by the city's efforts to tear down blighted properties and redevelop the area, Habitat for Humanity North Philadelphia (HFHNP) had assembled a series of parcels making up almost half of an entire city block. Harrison's efforts to understand how new home construction could be woven more closely into the neighborhood fabric caught HFHNP's attention.

In late 1998, Jon Musselman, construction manager for HFHNP, asked Harrison for help in developing a master plan for the block. Dubbed "Project 1800" because of the street address of the properties, the site encompassed the larger half of the block bounded by 18th and 19th streets and Montgomery Avenue and Gratz Street.

Design Process

Harrison began the design process with a series of community meetings involving representatives from HFHNP, Habitat families already in the neighborhood, and long-time residents. These "visioning sessions" identified several of the key issues that would shape the project, including the importance of front "stoops" at the street entrances, the need to accommodate parking on site, and the desire for more security over the rear spaces abutting the city's traditional mid-block alleys. The interviews also highlighted the challenge of accommodating modern, multi-generational families within the narrow (14 to 17 feet) widths of the traditional row house form found in the neighborhood.

Harrison and her design team developed a plan for the block that re-established the traditional continuity of row house façades (what Harrison calls "the street wall"), expanded the footprint of the new homes to one and a half times the width of the nineteenth-century module (22 feet), and converted the former alley and rear yards into a common space that could accommodate the required parking and provide space for play and informal social activity. The design called for new units to fill the gaps where homes had been demolished and renovations of the intact row homes that made up the balance of the Habitat-owned parcels.

Harrison's unit plans for the new homes featured small front porches recessed into the front façades (the "stoops" requested in the neighborhood meetings), large windows, and brick veneer on the street sides to match the neighboring homes. The ground floor plans featured living rooms on the street side and a kitchen/dining room space overlooking the rear garden and the common driveway court. The units could be built with three or four bedrooms and included an unfinished basement. Harrison worked closely with Musselman and the affiliate to make the interior spaces more "fluid and flexible" to respond to the feedback received via the neighborhood meetings.

As development of the unit and site plans progressed, architect Terry Jacobs became involved with the development of permitting and construction drawings while landscape architect John Collins worked with Harrison and Jacobs to develop details for the rear gardens and common driveway court.

Construction Process

Near the end of the design process Musselman brought Orleans Homebuilders, a successful suburban housing developer, into the project team. Orleans Homebuilders agreed to be the major project sponsor for Project 1800, bringing not only experienced construction volunteers to the project, but also extensive experience with prefabricated, panelized framing.

Prefabricated framing was a new approach for the affiliate, which heretofore had focused on renovating vacant shells or building one to two conventionally framed units at a time. Supported by Orleans Homebuilders' experienced crew, this approach gave Musselman and HFHNP the opportunity to try out a construction method they had been interested in for some time. "We wanted to explore how we could build these multiple unit infill projects as quickly as we could," notes Musselman, "and this approach enabled us to move a little more quickly."

While the site utilities and foundations were being completed, Orleans Homebuilders' crews were framing and sheathing the panelized components of the building shells in their suburban Philadelphia facility. Once the foundations were complete, these panels were trucked to the North Philadelphia site and craned in to place. Orleans' skilled crew of volunteers assembled them into completed shells in less than two weeks. Once this phase was complete, community volunteers and the new homeowners moved in to see the construction through to completion.

Project 1800 was completed in three phases of construction. The first two phases focused on construction of the new infill units and the final phase on the renovation of existing row house shells. The total project included seven three-bedroom homes of 1300 square feet, six four-bedroom homes of 1,400 square feet, one four-bedroom home with an accessible ground floor and private yard, and four rehabilitated row homes of varying sizes.

Lessons Learned

The eighteen homes completed in Project 1800 provided HFHNP with an important opportunity to rebuild a deteriorated city block and transform a neighborhood. The project has become the anchor of the affiliate's efforts in North Philadelphia. According to Harrison, crime rates have decreased and the influx of Habitat families has led to an increase in renovations and reinvestment by private owners, including several properties within the Project 1800 block.

Project 1800 also signaled a significant shift in HFHNP's strategy regarding the construction of new homes on vacant sites in the dense row house neighborhoods of Philadelphia. Rather than importing design strategies and exterior palettes from less dense suburban neighborhoods, the affiliate resolved to pattern its new houses after the traditional forms, materials, and design details derived from the surrounding homes.

The project also presented the project team with the opportunity to creatively respond to the city's parking requirement and the traditionally underutilized interior of the block. Rather than being subdivided into nineteen separate private yards, the common space at the interior solves the parking challenge and creates a second layer of community within the neighborhood. As one resident described it to Harrison, "I have my street neighbors and my backyard neighbors."

Originally designed by Harrison and Collins as a "space with rows of shade trees, solid fences and architectural paving," budget limitations led to asphalt paving and chain link to be substituted for the envisioned landscaping, fences, and pavers. Since the city would not maintain the "private" block interior, Harrison also felt that some form of property owners' association (POA) should be formed to care for and maintain the space. The POA idea was also rejected by the affiliate, although Musselman notes that he would establish a POA if the affiliate built a project with a shared commons area again.

Despite Harrison's fears that these decisions would lead to disuse and disrepair of this space, the interior court has evolved into a "robust contribution to the neighborhood." The children of the neighborhood have become the primary users of the space, which provides a generously paved alternative to the local streets for games of kickball and basketball, which can be overseen by parents from their kitchens and rear gardens.

At the unit design scale, Harrison observes that the front porches are well-used and the openness of the ground floor works well for the different families that live in the block. Expanding the width of the units to 22 feet has provided for social spaces large enough to accommodate family gathering. The unfinished basements, a high priority from the neighborhood input stage, were tagged as "expensive wasted space" during the budgeting phase of the project, and were only built because the city helped cover a portion of the costs. These spaces have proven to be "valuable, flexible space," observes Harrison. "We were glad the neighbors knew something we did not."

Though Harrison was involved in each phase of the project, her role tapered off during the final phases; and these homes saw some changes in the exterior materials used in the first phase of new construction (brick combined with stucco versus full brick on the street façades for example). Despite these changes, both Harrison and Musselman view the project as "very successful," citing the commitment to rebuilding with respect for the neighborhood scale and character, the innovative interior court, the unit plans, and the lessons learned from this first experience with panelized construction as the key dividends of the collaboration. Musselman notes that the affiliate viewed the interior court as "a gamble," but would use this approach again if faced with the opportunity to work on a similarly-scaled project.

Harrison believes that the key to the success of the project was the careful effort to study the neighborhood and explore new ideas for neighborhood redevelopment that preceded the planning of Project 1800. She also cites the effort to involve the surrounding neighbors in the pre-design visioning for the project as critical to articulating the key problems that would become the focus of the design team's efforts.

Musselman echoes this observation, and noted that the project also helped the affiliate learn creative ways to leverage the city's support for neighborhood revitalization into tangible and valuable design features—such as the city-funded basements. Musselman was also very pleased with the experience of panelized construction that "saved thousands of dollars" (over a conventional framing approach), but noted that "this would not have been possible without the help of an experienced partner like Orleans." Though no fully panelized homes have been built by HFHNP subsequent to this project, Musselman notes that several construction details and technologies introduced by Orleans Builders have migrated into the affiliate's construction standards on other projects, including the Stiles Street project profiled in Chapter 9.

sketch of common space at interior of block

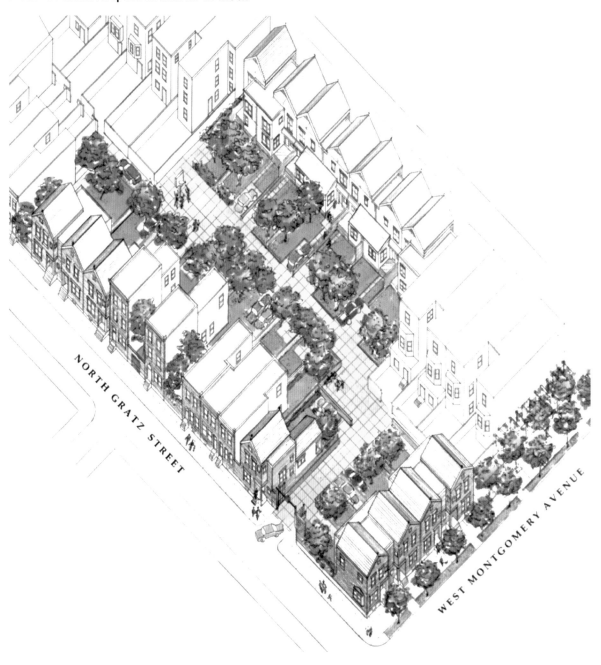

NORTH GRATZ STREET

WEST MONTGOMERY AVENUE

setting prefabricated wall panels

construction phase

site plan

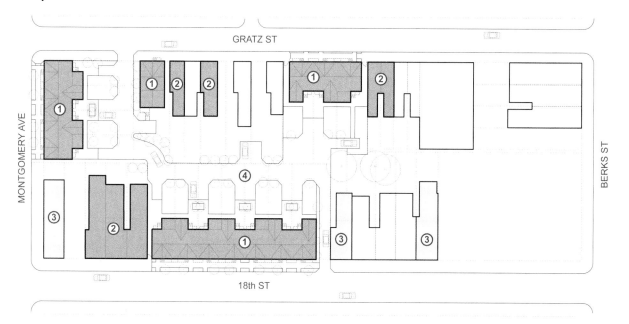

GRATZ ST

MONTGOMERY AVE

BERKS ST

18th ST

Key

1 - New Habitat Infill Units   **4** - Car Court
2 - Existing Shells Renovated by Habitat
3 - New Private Redevelopment

10'   40'   80'

view of common space at interior of block

typical unit floor plan

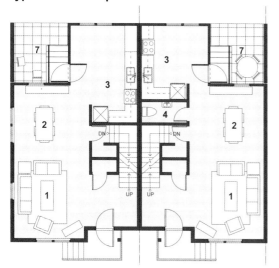

Ground Floor
(Basement Below)

Second Floor

Key

1 - Living

2 - Dining

3 - Kitchen

4 - Half Bath

5 - Bath

6 - Bedroom

7 - Porch

1'   5'   10'   20'

view of entry stoops

view from Gratz Street

Chapter 8

Roxbury Estates

Seattle, Washington
Olson Sundberg Kundig Allen Architects and Habitat for Humanity® Seattle/South King County (WA)

Key Partnerships

Rick Sundberg, architect and former principal at Olson Sundberg Kundig Allen Architects (OSKA)

Dorothy Bullit, executive director (2002–08), Habitat for Humanity Seattle/South King County (HFHSKC)

Marty Kooistra, executive director (2008–present), Habitat for Humanity Seattle/South King County (HFHSKC)

Program Summary

Two 2-bedroom, 1-bath, detached single-family units
800 square feet

Four 3-bedroom, 1-bath, detached single-family units
1,070 square feet

Two 4-bedroom, 2-bath, detached single-family units
1,450 square feet

Two 5-bedroom, 2-bath, detached single-family units
1,620 square feet

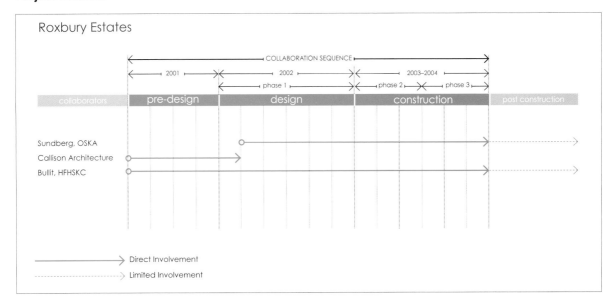

Catalysts for Collaboration

In 2001 the local Episcopal diocese donated a parcel of land in an urban residential neighborhood in Southwest Seattle to Habitat for Humanity Seattle/South King County (HFHSKC). The small parcel (less than an acre) was bounded by a busy arterial street to the south (S.W. Roxbury Street) and residential streets to the east and west. HFHSKC soon realized that developing the site would be challenging: the surrounding neighbors had concerns about the number of units that might be built there, and the affiliate had to accommodate the request of the diocese to reserve a housing unit for transitional housing.

Faced with a complex site and an ambitious building program, HFHSKC engaged Portland-based Callison Architecture to help develop a conceptual site plan for their building program. The conceptual site plan developed by Callison organized the housing into a single building, which provided small front yards and a large common yard and parking area on the interior of the property. This early work by Callison led HFHSKC to propose the construction of twelve housing units on the site to the City of Seattle.

Though the conceptual site plan successfully resolved Habitat's building program, families in the surrounding neighborhood—largely comprised of single-family homes—voiced opposition to the development of a single "large project" in the neighborhood. Efforts by HFHSKC and Callison to revise the site plan in response to the neighbors reduced the scale of the project below what HFHSKC thought they needed to build on the site. Facing the city's design review process and neighborhood concerns over the project, the affiliate was at an impasse.

Design Process

According to Rick Sundberg, then a principal of Olson Sundberg Kundig Allen Architects (OSKA) of Portland, the project arrived in his office via the firm's own employees, many of whom volunteered with HFHSKC. These young architects pitched the idea of taking on the project to the firm's principals. Sundberg and his colleagues agreed to the idea, though there was one caveat—as Sundberg recalls, "the only stipulation was that we try to do modern houses." With HFHSKC in agreement, Sundberg led the effort to carry out the design of the project, working with young members of the OSKA staff. The first challenge faced by OSKA was shepherding the project through the city design review process, which involved neighborhood review.

The City of Seattle's permitting process requires a design review for all multi-family projects in the city. At the time this project was under study, the Seattle building department was experimenting with ways to incorporate higher density in mixed-income, multi-family developments throughout the city. The Roxbury Estates site fell under the purview of this "pilot project" program, adding additional scrutiny.

Sundberg, very experienced with the city's design review process, was able to successfully navigate the project through community and city meetings for HFHSKC. However, this review process was not without impact on the design, Sundberg notes. Though the arrangement of the site originally proposed by Callison was largely retained, the city mandated that the building strategy change from a single building with twelve units to a group of ten single-family homes.

Working with Randy Allworth of Allworth Nessbaum Landscape Architects (who also donated design services), OSKA revised the site plan to organize a scheme featuring two-story houses along S.W. Roxbury Street, with one-story houses continuing the scale of the existing residential buildings on 24th Avenue S.W. and 25th Avenue

S.W. to the east and west respectively. A shared parking area and common lawn was designed to provide a play area for children while also providing access to smaller semi-private exterior spaces adjacent each home. As Sundberg recalls, "We tried to take a small project and add a small but bigger backyard communal space, then a semi-private back porch area, to layer the site with multi-scaled exterior spaces."

Though this revision appeased the community, it further increased the complexity of the city approvals process. As Sundberg recalls, "we had the ten houses and this [single] piece of property. We had to re-create lot lines and property lines for each one of them."

Sundberg recalls that he and his project director, Steven Wood, thought they were going to get a better break from the city in terms of submitting the drawings, but this would not be the case. Securing approvals from the city "took a lot longer than what we had planned on," observed Sundberg.

As the approvals process for the site proceeded, Sundberg and the OSKA team worked on the design of the ten house units. In considering the homes typically built by HFHSKC in the Seattle area, Sundberg recounts that the designs "recall 1920s era craftsman homes—single-family, single-story homes with a large front porch, sited on a typical urban lot." Sundberg and his design team wanted to develop home designs that would "engage a modern regional language," a design approach that has made OSKA one of Seattle's most recognized architecture practices. The team also focused on "bringing in natural light and air into the homes," and trying to "give them some volume," noted Sundberg.

OSKA also sought to create durable homes, with a proposed rain-screen cladding system utilizing fiber-cement panels. Though the designs did not incorporate any advanced energy conservation technologies, Sundberg notes that the homes had to meet the State of Washington Residential Energy Code, which is among the most progressive in the country. OSKA designed four different unit plans that are modest in floor area yet they innovate on common construction techniques. For example, the designs utilize butterfly roof configurations (rather than the more common gable roofs) resulting in increased interior volume in the homes. These tall spaces provided the opportunity to introduce more light into the spaces, as well as the opportunity to incorporate cross-ventilation strategies into the project. Construction of the houses began in 2003.

Construction Process

The decision to build ten individual houses posed some initial challenges. "It was a messy project getting all the foundations in," recalls Sundberg, due in part to a sloping topography on the site. The homes, all slab-on-grade, stick-framed construction, were framed on site with HFHSKC volunteers working alongside members of the OSKA design team.

Accustomed to working with skilled carpenters, the volunteer-based construction process of HFHSKC provided a useful lesson for the architects. As Sundberg recalls, "the houses are pretty typical in construction, except for the shed [roof] shapes exposed all the way through to the interior. That turned out more difficult for volunteer framers to do than trusses with flat ceilings." Bullit attests to Sundberg's recollection regarding the construction challenges faced by the volunteers, but notes that though "they were harder to build, they were kept on schedule." Though the projects were more complex than the designs normally built by HFHSKC, they also attracted "a lot of big donors who were inspired by the construction," said Bullit. "We got some good press because we were doing something unusual, a distinctive design … the project helped draw money, volunteers, and interest [which] helped to propel us to the next phase," Bullit observed.

Lessons Learned

For Sundberg, there were a number of valuable lessons learned on the project. The accommodations made for the neighborhood "allowed for a more nuanced site plan and contextually scaled series of buildings," he recalled. And though site design created a common space amenity for the families, it may have been "too ambitious," in Sundberg's view. This is a sentiment echoed by Bullit who noted that there was "minimal upkeep," of this space, and in the months following completion of the project the landscape was in need of an overhaul (which was done with Sundberg's assistance). Both recognized that there needed to be a better plan for the maintenance of the common space.

Though the OSKA design team was able to incorporate Habitat's standards into the design of the houses, the inability to interact with the homeowners was a challenge and a bit of a frustration. From Sundberg's perspective getting to interact with the families would allow the designers to respond to "the pressures of these folks, their lives, and how they are going to live in this place."

In Bullit's view the unconventional shape of the houses contributed to an increased amount of material waste on site and subsequently an increase in cost. The OSKA design team had researched the potential of incorporating prefabricated construction elements into the construction strategy, which Sundberg believes would have addressed this issue. "We thought we could design a much more efficient home and deliver it at probably even better cost," by utilizing prefabrication, but that approach "really moved outside of Habitat culture," observed Sundberg. "It is very important for Habitat to use volunteer labor."

By all accounts Roxbury Estates was a very successful project. Working within HFHSKC's budget of $51 per square foot, the OSKA design team transformed a common palette of materials into a rich configuration of buildings and exterior spaces. Bullit describes the Roxbury Estates homes as having "this airiness to them and elegance. The light was magnificent! There was a lot of dignity to the houses. The greatest triumph of the design was the way it honored the families that lived inside them," Bullit recalled.

Bullit attributes much of the success of the project to "a very good working relationship between the HFHSKC staff, OSKA, Callison, and the volunteers." She adds, "Both Callison and OSKA were willing to work with volunteers, which is a complicated way to do a building."[1]

site plan

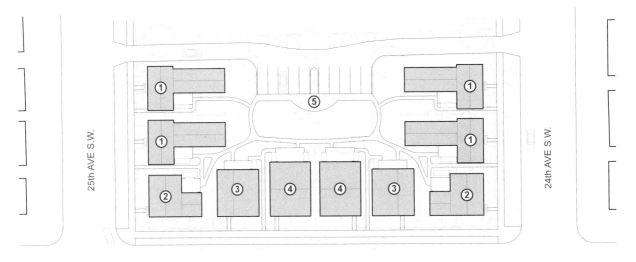

S.W. ROXBURY ST

Key

1 - 3 Bedroom   **4** - 5 Bedroom
2 - 2 Bedroom   **5** - Car Court & Common Area
3 - 4 Bedroom

view from S.W. Roxbury Street

view from S.W. Roxbury Street

view of entry porches

view of entry porches

floor plan—5 bedroom unit

Ground Floor

Second Floor

Key

1 - Living   **4** - Bath
2 - Dining   **5** - Bedroom
3 - Kitchen   **6** - Storage

view of living/dining room—2 bedroom unit

view of dining area, kitchen, and entry—2 bedroom unit

Chapter 9

Stiles Street Homes

Philadelphia, Pennsylvania
The Community Design Collaborative, Wallace, Roberts & Todd, and Habitat for Humanity® Philadelphia (PA)

Key Partnerships

Linda Dotter, and Beth Miller of the Community Design Collaborative (CDC)

Maarten Pesch, principal with Wallace, Roberts & Todd (WRT)

Megan McGinley, architect with Wallace, Roberts & Todd (WRT)

Jon Musselman, construction manager for Habitat for Humanity Philadelphia (HFHP)

Program Summary

Phase 1

Two 3-bedroom, 1-bath attached units

1,250 square feet

Five 4-bedroom, 1.5-bath attached units

1,495 square feet

Phase 2

Two 4-bedroom, 1.5-bath attached units

1,195 square feet

Project Timeline

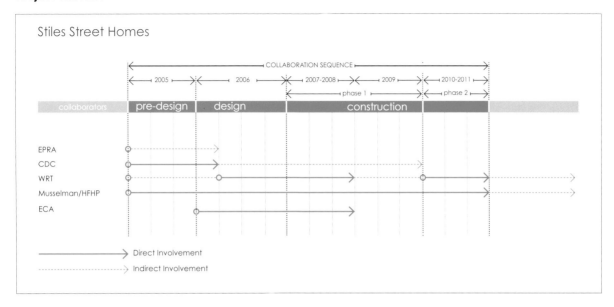

Stiles Street Homes

Catalysts for Collaboration

In 2001 Habitat for Humanity Philadelphia (HFHP) acquired several vacant properties in the Parkside neighborhood of West Philadelphia. Originally constructed early in the twentieth century, Parkside is characterized by larger than average (for Philadelphia) three- and four-story row homes with continuous front porches across the ground floor of each home. Though the neighborhood had declined in the latter decades of the twentieth century, it had retained a base of long-time residents. In the early 2000s Parkside was enjoying a modest renewal as young professionals migrated back from the suburbs to the still-affordable neighborhood.

In 2002, HFHP constructed the first two homes in Parkside as accessible units based on a two-story duplex configuration (known as a "twin" in Philadelphia) with side yards and off-street parking. When the affiliate began planning a further phase of construction in 2004, the newly formed East Parkside Residents' Association (EPRA) raised objections to further construction based on the model of the first two homes on the grounds that these homes were not compatible with the character and scale of the existing homes in the neighborhood. EPRA used its influence with the city to block further home construction on these sites until a compromise could be worked out.

Darren Edwards, a local architect and HFHP board member, suggested that HFHP seek assistance from the Community Design Collaborative (CDC) in developing a design approach that would be responsive to the neighborhood association's concerns. The CDC is a non-profit group that organizes teams of volunteers from the Philadelphia design community to provide pro-bono preliminary architectural, engineering, and planning services to non-profit organizations across the Philadelphia region.[1] The Collaborative agreed to help, and turned to Maarten Pesch of Wallace Roberts & Todd (WRT) to lead the volunteer team. Pesch and WRT were long-time CDC volunteers and brought significant affordable-housing design experience to the team. Pesch proposed to staff the balance of the team with young architects (led by Megan McGinley), landscape architects, and planners from within WRT, and the team began working with Jon Musselman and the HFHP board in the spring of 2005.

Design Process

Discussions with EPRA made it clear that the association wanted HFHP to build homes that would match the scale and character of the adjacent homes as closely as possible. In addition to this design challenge, the WRT team and HFHP identified these homes as a great opportunity to explore ways to incorporate sustainable design strategies into the affiliate's construction standards. With encouragement and a pledge of support from the Energy Coordinating Agency (ECA), a Philadelphia-based organization that promotes sustainable building technologies, the affiliate decided to pursue LEED® certification for the project as a pilot project under the US Green Building Council's LEED for Homes program.[2] According to Musselman, this decision was driven by a desire to lower the homeowners' energy costs, and the hope that the publicity associated with the LEED goal would attract donations to the project.

The three-story scale of the adjacent nineteenth-century homes presented a significant challenge to the affiliate, which was accustomed to building two-story units. The initial design studies developed by Pesch and the WRT team explored a broad range of alternative solutions for the unit designs illustrated by site plans, unit plans, and street elevation studies for each option. In addition, WRT developed a "design challenge matrix" to help Musselman and the HFHP board understand how their standard design approach and the goal of neighborhood compatibility compared across a broad spectrum of design decisions embedded in the project. The team also prepared a detailed study of the design and construction strategies the affiliate could use to meet the LEED certification goal. This study was presented to the HFHP board in December of 2005.

The study provided the basis for an agreement between the affiliate and the neighborhood association regarding the design of the units. The plan called for seven row house units, which would include several design features geared to EPRA's concerns, including: three-story high façades units at the street side, brick veneer on the steel elevations, continuous porches, and raised foundations. Mussleman and the affiliate retained WRT to carry the project forward through detailed design and construction.

Pesch and the WRT team began this next phase of the project with a day-long sustainable design planning effort involving the full project team, including the energy rating consultant from the ECA and representatives from the affiliate. This planning session established the specific design and construction strategies that would be incorporated into the project, including high insulation values, high-efficiency heating and air-conditioning systems, increased daylighting (via large windows at perimeter spaces and light tubes at interior spaces), bamboo flooring in place of carpet, and low-flow plumbing fixtures. In a key project decision, WRT and the affiliate decided to use an insulated concrete formwork (ICF) system to provide the key structural elements and the high insulation values for the exterior walls in a single system.

The unit configuration of the Stiles Street homes features a mix of four- and three-bedroom units. Each home has an unfinished basement, with the ground floor raised above the sidewalk level. The units have a partial third floor, created by a roof that slopes from three stories at the street to two stories at the rear. The ground floor of each unit has the kitchen positioned in the middle of the plan, which allows each family to choose to locate the living and dining spaces on either the street side or the side facing the rear yard.

Construction Process

HFHP decided to build the Stiles Street homes in two phases and began the construction in March of 2007. The decision to use ICFs for the perimeter walls posed two challenges for the team: construction of the wall system was beyond the scope of what could be constructed by volunteers (requiring paid labor) and, though only two homes were planned for completion in the initial phase, the ICF shells for all seven units needed to be constructed at one time. According to Musselman and Frank Monaghan, the affiliate executive director who arrived just as phase 1 was completed, this "presented a real strain on the affiliate's resources." Once the ICF system was complete, the balance of the construction was performed by a blend of affiliate volunteers, Habitat homeowners, and skilled tradesmen.

The first two units were completed in October 2008. These homes received a LEED Silver certification and were the first LEED-certified affordable-housing units completed in the Philadelphia region. The remaining five units were completed in the fall of 2009. A second phase of homes, two accessible units on the opposite side of Stiles Street (designed by WRT as well), completed in 2011.

Lessons Learned

The Stiles Street homes provided many lasting lessons for the WRT/HFHP team. According to Monaghan, the energy conservation strategies integrated in the homes have made a remarkable impact on homeowner utility costs. Monaghan estimates that the energy bills for these homes are approximately one quarter of what they see in their typical row house units—a "home run" in his view. Though the affiliate will use more volunteer-friendly structural systems (like wood framing) rather than ICFs, a number of the design and construction strategies utilized in these homes have become standard practice for the affiliate. These include high insulation values in walls and roofs, high-efficiency heating and air-conditioning systems, an emphasis on daylighting via larger windows and light tubes, water-efficient fixtures, and attention to the impact of solar orientation on choices regarding unit design. The affiliate has also adopted bamboo floors, utilized for the first time in the Stiles Street houses, as a standard. The bamboo floors result in better indoor air quality than carpet and, unlike carpet, can be installed by volunteers. By Monaghan's estimate these features add approximately 5–7 percent to the cost of construction, which is okay with Monaghan and HFHP: "now that we've seen the utility cost savings, we want to pass that along to all our homeowners."

In contrast, the accommodations made to satisfy the neighborhood association pushed the scale of the homes beyond what the affiliate can sustain. The seven units constructed in the first phase range from 1,250 square feet three-bedroom units to 1,495 square feet four-bedroom units—almost 24 percent larger than the standard home the affiliate builds in other areas of the city. If faced with the same pressure to build larger homes to match a surrounding context, Monaghan believes the affiliate would be forced to "step away from the site."

Fortunately, pressure from EPRA had eased by the time the second phase of units were planned. The two units designed by WRT for lots across the street from the first phase are four-bedroom units of only 1195 square feet, but employ many of the same responses to the neighborhood context, including the continuous porches and the three-story scale at the street. However, in an effort to bring costs down, the affiliate opted for fiber cement siding on the street façades rather than brick for these units, and omitted the basements on these homes.

HFHP also found that the LEED certification credential of the first homes brought lots of positive press, but did not produce the additional financial help they hoped for. Musselman noted that, though the affiliate will incorporate the green design features into their future projects, they would not pursue LEED certification again unless it was tied to financial support.

In the eyes of Musselman and Monaghan, the collaborations with WRT and the CDC have been very successful. According to Musselman, WRT's experience with large-scale affordable housing and sustainable design were "invaluable" and will have a lasting impact on the affiliate, and Monaghan notes, "we would not be where we are with green design today without WRT."

sketch of street view

site plan

STILES ST

42nd ST

GIRARD AVE

Key

1 - Phase One Units (7)
2 - Phase Two Units (2)
3 - Habitat Homes From 2002

10'   40'   80'

phase 1 construction showing ICF wall system

phase 1 construction

street view (phase 2 under construction)

typical unit floor plan

Ground Floor
(Basement Below)

Second Floor

Third Floor

Key

1 - Living
2 - Dining
3 - Kitchen

4 - Half Bath
5 - Bath
6 - Bedroom

7 - Attic
8 - Porch

1'   5'   10'   20'

phase 1 rear yards

phase 1 street view

view of stoop at sidewalk (phase 1)

Chapter 10

Stanley Street

Amherst, Massachusetts

Kuhn Riddle Architects, Amherst College, and Habitat for Humanity® Pioneer Valley (MA)

Key Partnerships

Chuck Roberts, principal, Kuhn Riddle Architects (KRA)

Tom Gerety, president, Amherst College

James Brassord, director of facilities, Amherst College

Tom Davies, assistant director of facilities/director of design and construction, Amherst College

M.J. Adams, executive director, Habitat for Humanity Pioneer Valley (HFHPV)

Michael Broad, building construction superintendent, Habitat for Humanity Pioneer Valley (HFHPV)

Charlie Klem, Habitat for Humanity Pioneer Valley (HFHPV)

Program Summary

House 1

3-bedroom, 1.5-bath detached unit

1,270 square feet

Houses 2–4

3-bedroom, 1.5-bath detached units

1,150 square feet

Project Timeline

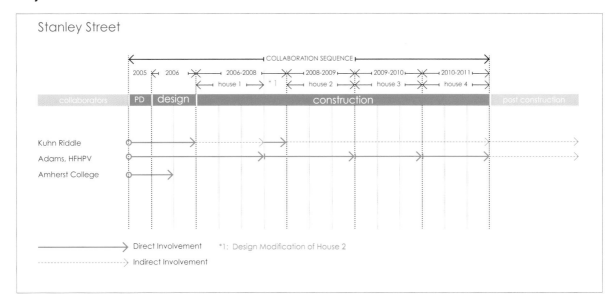

Stanley Street

COLLABORATION SEQUENCE

2005 — 2006 — 2006-2008 — 2008-2009 — 2009-2010 — 2010-2011

house 1 — *1 — house 2 — house 3 — house 4

collaborators | PD | design | construction | post construction

Kuhn Riddle
Adams, HFHPV
Amherst College

——————→ Direct Involvement   *1: Design Modification of House 2
·················→ Indirect Involvement

Catalysts for Collaboration

The Stanley Street homes are the result of a unique collaboration between Amherst College, Habitat for Humanity Pioneer Valley (HFHPV), and Kuhn Riddle Architects (KRA).

Located in the Connecticut River Valley of Western Massachusetts, HFHPV is situated within the "five colleges" region of the state (Amherst, Hampshire, Mount Holyoke, Smith College, and the University of Massachusetts Amherst). Amherst College, just across the Connecticut River from Northampton, provides a good deal of student volunteer support for HFHPV's building activities. Though the affiliate had been quite active in Northampton, lack of available affordable sites in nearby Amherst had prevented the affiliate from doing work there.

In the fall of 2005, Amherst College student and HFHPV volunteer, James Patchett, approached M.J. Adams, executive director of HFHPV, and offered to help find sites in Amherst. Adams and Patchett began to look at unused land held by Amherst College and the two identified a number of potential unused properties that appeared to be good candidates for HFHPV home sites.

Later that fall Patchett met with Amherst's president, Tom Gerety, and presented the idea of Amherst College donating land to HFHPV as well as the list of potential sites. As Adams recalls, Gerety was excited by the idea. His support drew other key staff at Amherst to the project. As Adams recalls "Once President Gerety was on board, we were able to find a champion on the facilities staff of the college." Jim Brassord, director of facilities for the college, was very involved in the physical plans for the campus and was in support of the proposal. Gerety carried the proposal to the Amherst College Board of Trustees, and in October they agreed to donate a parcel of land large enough for four homes to HFHPV. According to Patchett, the college gift came with the stipulation that the houses "complement the context of the site and its surrounding neighborhood," and that the building designs include enhanced energy conservation strategies. Brassord would act as Amherst College's representative on the project team.

Following the land donation, Brassord sought to involve local professionals on the project and soon approached KRA with the request to donate design services on the home design. In accepting the request, KRA was made aware of the college's design stipulations, and it was clear to Chuck Roberts, a principal at KRA and designated lead for the Stanley Street design team, that "these houses were going to challenge the perception of what a Habitat house typically is, and they were going to have a higher level of energy performance than anything they [HFHPV] had done before."

Design Process

The initial meeting between Brassord, KRA, and HFHPV sought to establish in "conceptual, broad brush terms" what the team was trying to accomplish before design commenced. For Roberts, the meeting was an opportunity for the team to set pragmatic goals (target levels of insulation, designing the house for solar energy collection, and so on), as well as for KRA to begin "familiarizing ourselves with the Habitat program." In Roberts' recollection of this first meeting, Brassord pushed the idea of super-insulating the houses, while HFHPV maintained its position to "build as green as we can with the resources we have on hand," with a minimum goal of Energy Star certification. KRA embraced these goals and began work on a number of alternative designs.

Following this initial meeting, the team (now including Michael Broad, HFHPV's building construction superintendent) met several more times to review

KRA's preliminary design proposals. The scheme that emerged from this process called for a three-bedroom house featuring a super-insulated "simple shed" building form, mirroring the vernacular farm structures common to the region. Amherst College signed off on this approach, and the design team turned its attention to the construction details of the home.

KRA and HFHPV utilized a second round of four to six meetings to refine the design to reflect what Roberts calls "volunteer build-ability." As Roberts recounts, the initial design proposal had several angled walls, which were met with a resounding "we are not going to build that" by the HFHPV Building Committee (comprised largely of the crews managing HFHPV job sites). Adams recounts that Roberts was "great at working through the criticism and understanding the necessity for simplifying the plan."

As the team moved forward, they sought input from both the adjacent community and from local building professionals experienced with construction of super-insulated homes. The team learned that, due to the insulation strategy, a single point source heater was all that would be required to heat the house, a significantly smaller (and more efficient) HVAC system than customary for HFHPV homes. For Adams, this represented a real advantage for the homeowners, many of whom "are moving out of a rental situation where they have never paid utilities independently before."

HFHPV was quick to notify KRA that the site had a high water table, ruling out basements. KRA suggested that they build exterior storage sheds connected to the main house, creating "exterior breezeways" and complementing the shed forms of the house. In siting the houses, KRA was careful to organize the house plans to take advantage of the solar orientation of the sites. As Roberts explains, "we lined the long axis east to west, and that allowed us to open up the long southern side of the house for solar gain. The roof is also pitched in that direction as well which was optimum for photovoltaic systems."

KRA also sought to overcome the "small house/small spaces" shortcoming they saw in HFHPV's typical home designs. As Roberts recounts, "We wanted to create a house that felt like it had an open plan. The houses are very small [in floor area]. If you start cutting up living rooms, dining rooms, and kitchens, you just end up with a bunch of little spaces." As a response, KRA created an open ground floor and connected the "public spaces" of the ground floor to the "private spaces" of the upper floor with the vertical volume of the stairway. This decision also supported the KRA design team's goal of a house infused with views to the countryside and natural light. Roberts describes the intended experience as "coming in the front entrance and seeing the view through the main volume … seeing the views to the south, and the indirect [north] light flowing down from the stairs. That draws you up at the same time you are drawn into the larger volume of the house."

Construction Process

Construction began on the first of the four houses in October of 2006, which was completed in January of 2008. The first house served as an opportunity to evaluate the design and the construction approach, and as Roberts and Adams recount, a number of issues emerged from this analysis. The first was that the house area had crept beyond the target size by 120 square feet, something both Adams and Roberts describe as "an oversight." Additionally, framing of the roof proved to be more difficult than expected. In response, KRA simplified the building volumes in order to address the framing issues and refined the plans to remove the area from the main building while retaining the overall relationship with the storage building. The changes appear negligible, according to Adams.

Based on this revised design HFHPV constructed three additional homes to complete the Stanley Street plan at a pace of about one house per year. The second Stanley Street home was completed in 2009, and the fourth and final home was completed in 2011.

Taking advantage of the solar orientation KRA considered when siting the homes, HFHPV has been able to equip all four of the houses with roof-mounted 25 KW photovoltaic (PV) arrays to provide electrical power for the homes, supplementing the power drawn from the electric utility company (and sometimes generating a surplus of power). The families are taking advantage of the house orientation in other ways. As Adams describes, "the families are setting up their homes so you actually walk out into a little garden area outside their sliding glass doors. So it's almost as if there is this merging of interior and exterior space, so even though the homes are small, they don't feel small."

The attention to solar orientation, the compact form of the houses, and the super-insulated envelope strategy have made the Stanley Street houses very energy efficient. The first house earned a score of 34 on the Home Energy Rating System (HERS) Index, well exceeding the original HFHPV goal of Energy Star (an 85 or lower).

As Adams is quick to point out, though the homes "do look a little different than the other houses in the neighborhood—and really stood out when the first one was built. Now there is a neighborhood of four of them. They are highly visible, and we really get extraordinary compliments on how beautiful the homes are, and how terrific it is that affordable housing can be so elegant." Though the reaction to the homes has been predominantly positive, Roberts also notes that some within the community have described the homes as "too nice for affordable housing," saying, "They look too designed."

Lessons Learned

The Stanley Street homes have provided many lessons that both KRA and HFHPV have transferred to subsequent projects. In Roberts' view, foremost among the lessons was the value of the extensive conversations with KRA had with the HFHPV construction team early on—"before we designed anything." The multiple work sessions with the affiliate staff were, in Roberts' assessment, critical to establishing a common set of objectives for the project within the project team. As Adams artfully states, "while it is joyful to be on a construction site building a home, it's also an extremely rewarding experience to be sitting around a table rolling out blueprints, talking through issues, and realizing that other people have different levels of technical understanding." The effort to integrate the knowledge and experience of the whole team, she notes, led to "something that worked really well and satisfied all the parties."

The Stanley Street homes were a "pioneering experience" for both KRA and HFHPV with regard to understanding how to make HFHPV homes more energy efficient, notes Roberts. KRA is currently working with HFHPV on new home designs, and the strategies honed on the Stanley Street homes have migrated to this new work. According to Roberts, "all of the houses HFHPV builds now are super-insulated and very air-tight, have minimal HVAC systems, and aim to utilize PV when they have the opportunity."

The success of the Stanley Street homes has impacted HFHPV in other ways. According to Adams, though HFHPV has "always had very good standing with the community as a small developer doing the right thing for affordable housing, this [project] has really lifted our credibility to the point where now private developers are giving us property to build affordable homes when they have an obligation to [incorporate affordable units] as part of their subdivision approval." Adams recounts the story of attending an Amherst planning meeting where a local for-profit developer was seeking approval for a housing development that included (as required in the local ordinance) lots reserved for affordable units. When asked by the planning board about his plans for these units, Adams said that the developer "turned and looked at me and asked 'You're with Habitat right?' I said 'Yes.' 'You're the one building the Stanley Street project?' and I said 'Yes.' 'Do you want a lot to build more houses on?' I said 'Yes!' We ended up with a building lot from that."

From Roberts' perspective the collaboration has been rewarding and fulfilling. As noted above, KRA continued to be involved with HFHPV on subsequent projects, and has also applied the lessons from this project to a winning proposal for a HFH-sponsored design competition. In his view, the most critical catalyst in this project was the conditions Amherst College attached to their land donation. In his view it is hard to imagine that this project could have come about without that mandate to "try something new and aim high."[1]

site plan

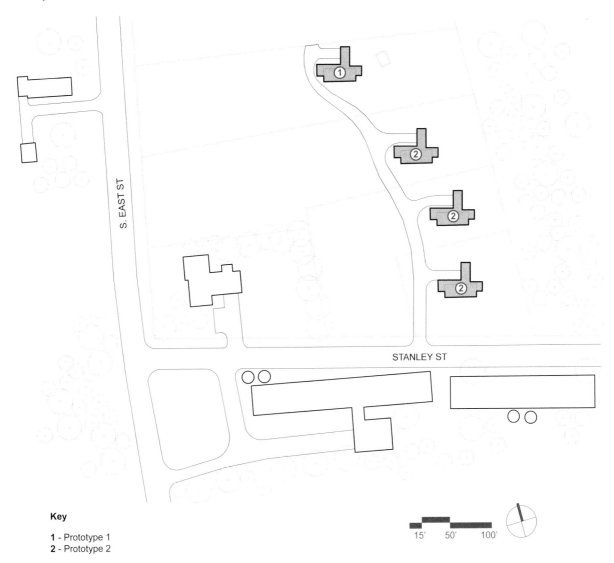

Key

1 - Prototype 1
2 - Prototype 2

S. EAST ST

STANLEY ST

15' 50' 100'

rendering of homes in site

view of house 1 from S. East Street

view of house 2

floor plan of house 1

Key

1 - Living   **4** - Half Bath   **7** - Storage
2 - Dining   **5** - Bath
3 - Kitchen   **6** - Bedroom

1'   5'   10'   20'

view of dining area and kitchen

Chapter 11

New Columbia Villa

Portland, Oregon

Paul McKean Architecture, LLC and Habitat for Humanity® Portland/Metro East (OR)

Key Partnerships

Kim Pannan, intern, Boora Architects, LLC

Paul McKean, principal, Paul McKean Architecture, LLC

Sky Khalsa, construction manager, Habitat for Humanity Portland/Metro East (HFHP)

Steve Messinetti, executive director, Habitat for Humanity Portland/Metro East (HFHP)

Program Summary

Five 3-bedroom, 2-bath detached units

1,140 square feet

Project Timeline

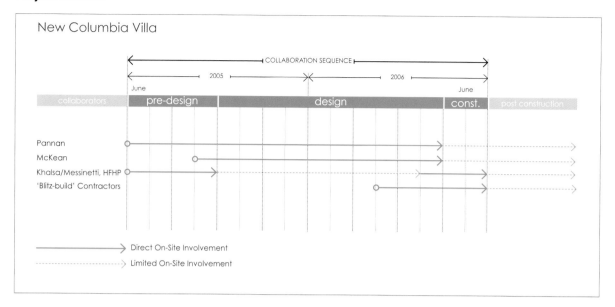

New Columbia Villa

| collaborators | pre-design | design | const. | post construction |

Pannan
McKean
Khalsa/Messinetti, HFHP
'Blitz-build' Contractors

Direct On-Site Involvement
Limited On-Site Involvement

Catalysts for Collaboration

Kim Pannan moved to the United States from Australia in 2003 to pursue her architectural career via an internship with Boora Architects in Portland, Oregon. Soon after settling in Portland, Kim began working as a volunteer with Habitat for Humanity® Portland/Metro East (HFHP). Pannan found that many in the affiliate shared her interest in sustainable design, including the affiliate's lead construction manager, Sky Khalsa. Pannan soon become involved with several HFHP committees, including the construction and family support committees, and was a regular volunteer on Habitat construction sites.

Several of the homes Pannan helped build had been designed by local architects. Although she admired the design of the units, she felt they were not well tuned to the needs of the affiliate's homebuilding process. "It struck me that these houses were rather complicated, given that they were to be constructed with volunteer labor," she observed. It required almost eighteen months for the affiliate to complete the homes, and Pannan became convinced that she could come up with a better solution. "It just struck me that [the design approach for these homes] was pretty inefficient," said Pannan. "I wanted to find a way to simplify it all."

Pannan began to test her ideas for a simpler approach via entries in two affordable-housing design competitions, one based in Portland and one in Australia. Both competitions focused on compact, flexible, and efficient solutions for homes to be built on small urban lots. The process of developing submissions (in partnership with two young architect colleagues) convinced Pannan that the Portland affiliate could "get more bang for their buck," if they could build homes that utilized a similar approach.

Pannan showed her competition submissions to HFHP's design committee, and according to Pannan, "they pricked up their heads straight away and said that looks great." HFHP had just purchased five lots within a new planned housing development in north Portland, New Columbia Villa (NCV), and they asked Pannan to develop designs for these new homes.

Design Process

Pannan assembled a team of seven young intern architects from different firms in Portland. Paul McKean, a member of the design team who had recently opened his own practice, agreed to serve as the "architect of record" (the architect responsible to the city for code compliance of the design).

NCV was planned by the Housing Authority of Portland as a "Hope VI" (mixed-income) development containing more than 800 homes. All homes built within the new neighborhood had to conform to the NCV design guidelines that, according to McKean, "were basically trying to promote construction of 'Portland bungalows,'" one of the most common house styles found in the city's pre-World War II neighborhoods.

All proposed home designs for the development had to be approved by a design review panel appointed by the city to oversee projects within NCV before construction could begin. According to Pannan, securing approval from the design review panel meant that the team would have to "design a very high-quality piece of building that did not stand out as a Habitat for Humanity house."

The team also realized that their belief that "good design could and should be simple and efficient to construct" would be put to the test when the NCV sites were selected for the Habitat for Humanity Home Builders Blitz program. This would be HFHP's first attempt at a Home Builders Blitz build, and their plan called for the professional builders to complete the homes over a seven-day period in June. Four homes would be constructed in the blitz build, each by a different team of home builders. The fifth lot would be used as a staging site during the blitz week, with the house on that site to be built later by the affiliate. "We knew this would really test our theory," noted Pannan.

The Home Builders Blitz program also meant that the traditional emphasis on designing homes that would be "volunteer friendly" (easy to build by unskilled volunteers) would shift to a different emphasis, according to Steve Messinetti, executive director of HFHP: "In this case the challenge was to design a house that would be 'friendly' for this blitz."

With the support of their respective employers, the design team began work on the project, largely after hours and on weekends. Pannan served both as coordinator of the design team and as the liaison to the affiliate. Sky Khalsa gave the team their initial briefing, explaining the affiliate's goals for the project, emphasizing HFHP's interest in integrating sustainable design strategies and construction standards into the project, and explaining the special issues associated with designing for a blitz build. The team met regularly to share their developing design ideas and presented updates to the affiliate's design committee on a monthly basis.

The design team presented a variety of design configurations to the affiliate over the following months, seeking to find a balance between HFHP's needs and the requirements of the NCV design guidelines. "We did two or three designs that were much more modern," notes McKean, but when these preliminary schemes were shown to the NCV design review board they were quickly rejected. "The affiliate was open to something more modern," said McKean, "but we realized we would have to take the city's guidelines more seriously."

The design that emerged from this process featured a common plan for each of the five units. The team felt that "porches were very important for creating neighborhoods," said McKean, and the plan for the NCV homes featured a large porch on the street side and rear of the house. The social spaces (living room, kitchen, and dining area) were arrayed in an open configuration on the south side of the plan to take advantage of the stronger daylight on that exposure. The three bedrooms and two baths were configured along the north side of the plan with a zone of closets and "storage boxes" providing a buffer between the bedrooms and the common areas. "There is virtually no hallway in the plan," said McKean. "They are really quite efficient."

In addition to small variations in the placements of windows, the team developed a range of exterior color palette options (which could be selected by the homeowners) to provide variation between the units, which were to be located on adjacent lots. The team also proposed to stagger the home setbacks to provide variety between the homes "and provide some relief in the streetscape," notes Pannan.

While the prospective homeowner families were being selected by HFHP during the design process, they were not directly involved in the design process. However, one of the selected families included a disabled child, and the team met with that family to customize the standard plan with an entrance ramp and accessible bathroom.

After receiving approval from HFHP, the team presented the scheme to the NCV design review board. In the initial presentation, the identical plans and exterior configurations proposed for all five houses were rejected by the board. According to Pannan, the review board felt that the homes should have more variation than the proposed range of color schemes would provide.

The team quickly regrouped and developed a range of roof configurations (that is gable roofs and hipped roofs) and porch details that gave each house a different look, but preserved the common floor plan. The second submission received the review board's approval.

Construction Process

Under Habitat's Home Builders Blitz program, each of the sponsoring home builders provides all the materials and labor for their assigned house and is responsible for planning their own strategy for building and soliciting material donations for the homes. The building teams for the NCU project ranged from companies that focused on standard development-grade homes to companies that built mostly "high-end" custom homes. According to Pannan, each team brought a unique strategy to the project, "and a unique attitude toward the designs."

The design team began meeting with representatives from the four building teams as soon as the design approach began to take shape, and the builders gave lots of feedback on the schemes. "We thought we had designed the simplest possible houses," said Pannan, "but that was not the builders' impression!"

The primary focus of the builders' feedback were changes to construction details aimed at speeding up the construction and minor adjustments related to accommodating donated materials like windows and doors. The primary design change was the addition of a support post at the corner of the front and rear porches where the design team had planned for a cantilever.

The plans for the blitz build week did not call for the design team to be on site, but Pannan and Paul McKean planned to visit the site mid-morning on Saturday, the first day of construction. The building teams started at 7 a.m. and when Pannan and McKean arrived on site they found the homes almost completely framed. "We almost missed it," said Pannan. "I've never seen anything like it." The excitement of seeing many months of work being constructed was "a real adrenaline rush," said Pannan. She and McKean spent the whole day on site answering questions from builders about construction details and "our design intentions."

Naturally, each builder also wanted to be the first to complete their home. This competition to build quickly "led some builders to take some short cuts," in Pannan's view, "and this resulted in a noticeable difference in the final results." According to McKean, he and Pannan made sure to call important issues to Sky Khalsa's attention, but left decisions about how to respond up to him. "That was his call," said McKean. "We were working for him."

One building team made a special impression on Pannan for their commitment to quality and for their efforts to "follow the plans to the letter." Early on this builder appeared to be moving at the slowest pace, stopping frequently to discuss details with Pannan and McKean. In the end, notes Pannan, this team had fewer mistakes to correct and their house was finished first. "It was a bit like the tortoise and the hare," observed Pannan, "but their house was really a work of art."

Lessons Learned

From Pannan's view, one of the biggest challenges of the design process was managing the time and efforts of the volunteer design team. "We had a team of very good-willed people working on their own time and I did not want to abuse that," observed Pannan. According to Pannan, the most difficult part of the leadership role was finding the right balance between allowing each architect "some free rein" to contribute to the design and making sure the team did not work too inefficiently. "There were a few points," according to Pannan, "where something [a team member] had spent a good bit of time on was not used," which resulted in some tension within the team.

Managing that process involved a big learning curve for me," she observed. "In hindsight, the team I put together was too big, and I ended up spending more time managing the process than the project." The fact that the design volunteers came from multiple offices also made the effort to coordinate communications more challenging. "This would have been easier if all the team worked one office," she said. McKean agrees, adding, "These houses are just too small to have seven people developing construction drawings."

In Pannan's view the most important factor contributing to the success of the project was her prior experience as a volunteer builder and committee member within the HFHP affiliate. "Understanding how Habitat worked across the board was very important," she said.

Despite these challenges, Pannan was very pleased with the experience. "The good will of everyone involved, and the satisfaction of seeing families move into the houses, made the many months of effort and the hours of negotiations over design all worthwhile," she said.

McKean feels the same. "I'd love to do this again," he said. McKean also notes that working with clients like Habitat requires architects to temper their expectations with regard to the level of control over the details that they enjoy on conventional projects. "There is no point in specifying every detail," he said. "People are constantly donating materials and you just can't control that kind of stuff."

In Messinetti's view, the NCV homes presented a challenging set of overlapping stakeholders and project goals that made the task facing the design team more complex than most prior projects built by HFHP: meeting the city's design standards and blending into the mixed-income development, understanding the special challenges of the blitz build approach, managing the input of the four professional home builders, advancing the affiliate's sustainable building standards; all the while remaining faithful to the needs of the homeowner families and to Habitat's mission. "The design team had plenty on their plate," he observed.

The results "met everyone's goals," according to Messinetti. "The homeowners were thrilled … the city was very excited with the way these projects turned out … the builders were pleased with the experience … and these were the greenest homes the affiliate had built and we've built on what we learned on subsequent projects. This project was a big boost for the affiliate—we got a great deal out of working with this team."[1]

site plan

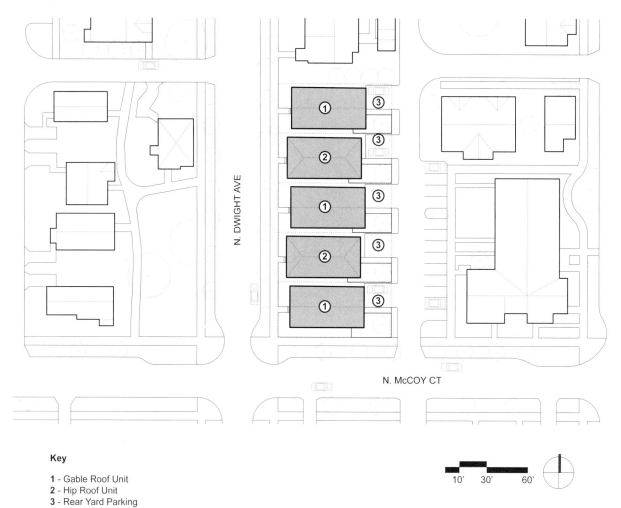

Key

1 - Gable Roof Unit
2 - Hip Roof Unit
3 - Rear Yard Parking

10'   30'   60'

street elevation with proposed color schemes

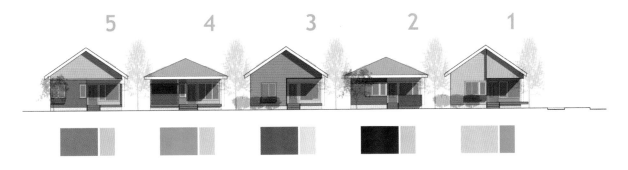

view from alley—gable roof unit

view of entry—gable roof unit

view from street—hipped roof unit

typical floor plan

Key

1 - Living
2 - Dining
3 - Kitchen
4 - Bath
5 - Bedroom
6 - Porch

1'   5'   10'   20'

view from street—gable roof unit

view from street—hipped roof unit

dedication ceremony

Chapter 12

Webster Street

Portland, Oregon

Scott Mooney, David Posada, and Habitat for Humanity® Portland/Metro East (OR)

Key Partnerships

Scott Mooney, intern architect, THA Architects

David Posada, intern architect, GBD Architects

Carmen Schleiger, director of housing development, Habitat for Humanity Portland/Metro East (HFHP)

Steve Messinetti, executive director, Habitat for Humanity Portland/Metro East (HFHP)

Dick Hutchinson, Walsh Construction Co.

Howard Thurston, structural engineer, New Paradigm Engineering

Program Summary

One 2-bedroom, 1-bath detached unit

900 square feet

One 4-bedroom, 2-bath detached unit

1,250 square feet

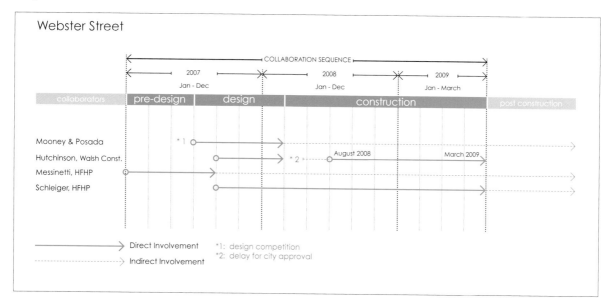

Webster Street

Catalyst for Collaboration

Each year, the Cascadia Green Building Council (a regional chapter of the US Green Building Council (USGBC)) sponsors a regional component of the "Natural Talent Design Competition," a national program sponsored by the USGBC to promote "creative thinking by students and young professionals" regarding projects and ideas for sustainable building in their communities.[1]

In 2006, the Cascadia Green Building Council approached Habitat for Humanity Portland/Metro East (HFHP) with a request to use one of the affiliate's undeveloped sites and the affiliate's typical Habitat home standards (floor area, and so on) as the subject of the competition. According to Steve Messinetti, executive director of HFHP, though there was no commitment by the affiliate to build the winning entry, it presented an opportunity to learn from the competition entries and to gain positive exposure for HFHP's efforts in the East Bay area. In January of 2007 the Cascadia Green Building Council opened the competition to the public. The competition brief called for design proposals for simple, decent, affordable duplex homes (two bedroom and four bedroom) that would meet USGBC LEED® Homes Silver certification requirements.

Scott Mooney and David Posada, classmates at the University of Oregon and intern architects working for different Portland architectural firms, decided to enter the competition together. Another intern architect, Kathy Bush, was part of the design team early on, but had to pull back due to other commitments. Working at different firms meant that much of the work on the competition entry occurred outside of normal office hours. Working nights and weekends, the two developed a design proposal that aimed to exceed the competition brief and target LEED for Homes Platinum certification, which they submitted in April.

Following the competition entry deadline, the Cascadia Green Building Council competition jury members met with HFHP to get the affiliate's feedback on the competition entries. In June, the jury announced that Mooney and Posada were awarded first place for the region. Mooney and Posada recollect that though winning the regional competition was exciting (their design would be forwarded to Chicago for the national phase of the Natural Talent Design Competition), "even more exciting was that the Cascadia Green Building Council handed over the designs to Habitat for Humanity for review to see if they were interested in pursuing any of them as an actual project."

Messinetti recalls that the winning design by Mooney and Posada was very interesting to the affiliate, but also a bit "ambitious" with regard to the extent of design innovations the design team used to achieve the LEED for Homes Platinum goal. Though HFHP had recent experience in green building, notably the New Columbia Villa Project, profiled in Chapter 11, they had not pursued LEED certification for any of their buildings, and certainly not one aiming this high. As the affiliate deliberated as to whether or not to move forward with the duplexes, Walsh Construction was brought into the discussion.

Walsh Construction, a local construction company, was in the fourth year of a five-year commitment to build one home a year for HFHP. Dick Hutchinson, HFHP's primary liaison with Walsh Construction, was asked to evaluate the design as candidate for the company's fifth Habitat home. As Hutchison recalls, the project seemed to fit well with the goals that had framed their five-year commitment to HFHP, in particular the goal to "implement and learn how to build systems that are green and sustainable." Walsh Construction said "yes" to constructing the houses. Recognizing that the cost of the two houses would exceed

Walsh's corporate commitment, Messinetti sought sponsorship from other local businesses and past partners, and the Bank of America came forward with both construction volunteers and a $75,000 funding commitment.

Design Process

In the fall of 2007, Mooney, Posada, Messinetti, Hutchinson, and Carmen Schleiger, director of housing development for HFHP, began the first of a series of meetings that would refine the project goals and the design. As Mooney and Posada recall, "it was clear that there were a lot of questions on the table with regard to what's realistic, or what really works." As the affiliate and Mooney and Posada recall, Walsh Construction was instrumental in providing feedback based upon their experience in green building practices. From these initial discussions Mooney and Posada completed an initial round of revisions focused upon reducing the window-to-wall ratios and simplifying the plan and roof forms. In Mooney and Posada's opinion, "the scheme held up pretty well."

As revisions to the drawings progressed, the team continued pre-construction phase meetings to discuss construction details, material choices, and track LEED credits. These meetings also provided opportunities for charrettes with local green building experts, who weighed in on the team's approach to systems and assemblies. From Mooney and Posada's perspective, it was critical to have the LEED for Homes provider, Rebecca Novis of Green Hammer Construction, involved in the design process and team meetings.

Many of these pre-construction phase meetings, as Hutchinson recounts, involved the team discussing "very idealistic, innovative, pioneering ideas" for the materials and systems to be used in the house. The meetings provided an opportunity for the team to discuss the design and get feedback from the various perspectives represented on the design team. As Hutchinson recalls, Mooney and Posada were receptive to this process and each side taught the other. "They were very willing to listen to my concerns about what's practical and affordable, and I was willing to stretch my zone of comfort and try many, many new things in this building," said Hutchinson.

Over the next eighteen months, Mooney and Posada worked to integrate the comments and suggestions of HFHP and Walsh Construction into the design scheme. The final design closely resembled the competition entry in terms of its massing, orientation, and organization on the site, factors that, as Posada recalls, "really contributed to its performance." The final scheme utilized radiant heating in exposed concrete floor slabs, 2 × 6 Optimum Value Engineered (OVE) wall framing with exterior rigid insulation, Structural Insulated Panel System (SIPS) (for the roof decks), metal roofing, two rainwater collection cisterns for summer irrigation, and wood fiber cement block walls. Walsh Construction leveraged its extensive contacts in the local building community to get many of these systems at a reduced cost. Though the houses originally were designed with photovoltaic arrays, donors for these systems could not be found.

In March of 2008, following a considerable effort to refine the plans and details, Mooney and Posada handed the drawings to Walsh Construction, who shepherded them through the permit process with the city. At this point the decision to change from a duplex to two separate single-family houses (a 900 square feet two-bedroom and a 1,250 square feet four-bedroom) came to impact the permit process. The site had not been legally divided into two parcels. This oversight required a delay to complete the subdivision process (handled by HFHP), and a revision of the drawings to indicate the new property lines and setbacks for the proposed houses.

Though this oversight cost the team some time, another set of issues was also promising to delay the construction process. The City of Portland's plan reviewers expressed concerns over both the SIPS roof panels and the wood-fiber cement block walls, materials unfamiliar to the reviewers. After the team provided engineering data and additional manufacturing data to satisfy the city's concerns, building permits for the two houses were issued in late August of 2008.

Construction Process

Walsh Construction began the long-awaited construction of the two houses in September of 2008. As part of their commitment to HFHP, Walsh provided an on-site construction manager, Thea Zander, for the duration of the construction phase. As construction began, the extensive pre-construction arrangements for donated materials began to pay off in ways that helped the project realize its sustainable construction goals. A sampling of the donated materials included FSC-certified framing lumber, standing seam metal roofing, wood-chip insulated concrete forms (locally produced with recycled wood fiber), SIPS panels, fiberglass windows, marmoleum floors in the kitchen and bathrooms, and wool carpets in the bedrooms. Concrete salvaged from demolition sites was reused for landscape pavers.

The construction of the homes relied heavily upon skilled laborers that Walsh Construction had organized. However, Zander made sure to organize volunteer build days around "volunteer-friendly" construction phases. As Hutchinson notes, the homeowners were able to get their "sweat equity" time in on-site during the framing and finishing phases.

HFHP, Walsh Construction, and the Cascadia Green Building Council all worked to ensure the project had a high profile in the local media, which translated into donations of time and materials for the team. The architects made their own contribution to the media attention given the project when they hosted a small concert to raise money to pay for a locally produced, no-VOC paint for the house (Yolo Colorhouse Paint).

Construction was completed in March of 2009, and the homes underwent final testing and certification reviews. Both homes achieved LEED for Homes Platinum certification in April of 2009, making them the first LEED for Homes Platinum project certified in the State of Oregon.

Lessons Learned

In HFHP's eyes Webster Street served as a one-of-a-kind project—outside the bounds of their normal standards, but a valuable opportunity to gain experience with several promising non-traditional materials and systems and advance their understanding of sustainable design and construction.[2] "It was an extraordinary project for us," recalls Messinetti. "At the end of the day, we knew there were a lot of things in there that we wouldn't be able to do on other houses, but … this was a demonstration project for us."

The partnership with Walsh Construction was the critical piece of the puzzle that enabled these homes to be built. As the designers note, "the primary reason we got the opportunity to develop this design and really see it through as a LEED Platinum Habitat home was because of the relationship that Habitat had with Walsh Construction."

From HFHP's perspective, the Webster Street homes raised and answered a number of questions. For example, the concrete slab on grade with embedded hydronic heating proved to be too far from the norm for the affiliate to replicate. Messinetti notes, however, that the project has "moved us in the direction of exploring other options for heating and cooling the homes." For Mooney and Posada the reaction to the hydronic floor heating was one among many instructive lessons. As Posada observed, "I think it's important for people with our level of experience to recognize that the things that young architects get excited about are not always the same things that homeowners get excited about." Mooney added, "So one of the things we heard back from Habitat was that the family asked HFHP for the okay to cover the exposed concrete floor with carpet or wood. So, we learned that to a mom with two kids having a stained concrete floor is not necessarily a desirable feature."

Another lesson the team took from the project related to the foray into wood-fiber cement walls and SIPS roof panels. Though the systems were not new to the Portland area (Mooney and Posada recollect that a local building had utilized SIPS for wall construction), their application as roof systems was novel to the city. The team learned that earlier involvement of the parties granting approvals would be prudent when using new technologies on future projects.

The LEED for Homes Platinum certification is a source of pride for HFHP. However, as Schleiger notes, "the biggest deterrent to doing another LEED project is all the certification and paperwork." Consequently HFHP has shifted from pursuing LEED and Energy Star certification to a less documentation-intensive system called Earth Advantage Homes®, a program developed by the Earth Advantage Institute.[3]

Hutchinson's perspective offers insight into the collaborative nature of the team. As he notes, this project demonstrated that "a successful project can result from an idealistic innovative design [being] brought to a team of builders and to a Habitat affiliate with a good cooperative attitude." Echoing Hutchinson's sentiments, Messinetti credits Mooney and Posada's "flexibility and patience" as well as "how open they were with advice and making changes and really working through the process."

Mooney and Posada credit the process of working with Hutchinson and Schleiger with making the project a stronger solution, and a more carefully integrated design. "We were able to skim off a lot of the extra gear and extra stuff that sometimes gets added on a green project and really try to stay true to the idea of responding to the site itself, the solar orientation, lot orientation and view, and where people would want to sit on the porch and things like that. So I think the stuff that contributes hopefully to people's appreciation or enjoyment of the place was an essential part of the design, not an add-on," observes Mooney.

site plan

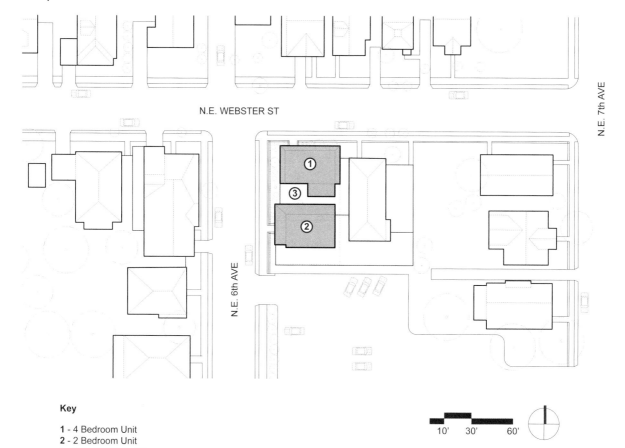

N.E. WEBSTER ST

N.E. 6th AVE

N.E. 7th AVE

Key

1 - 4 Bedroom Unit
2 - 2 Bedroom Unit
3 - Shared Courtyard

10'   30'   60'

aerial view of homes

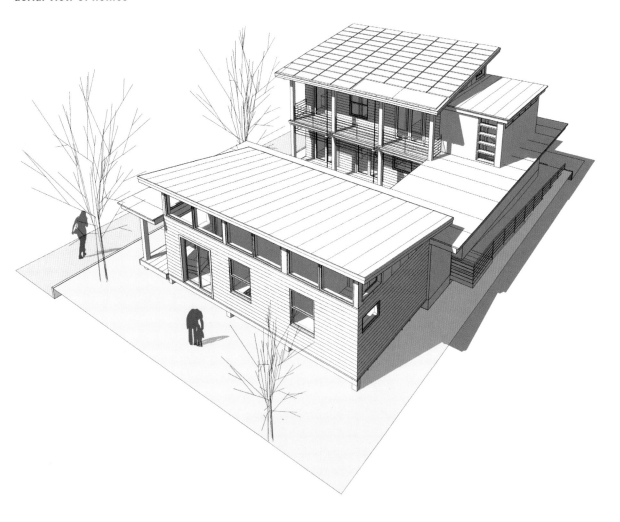

section diagram of houses and courtyard

view of entry (two-bedroom house)

view of entry (four-bedroom house)

floor plan

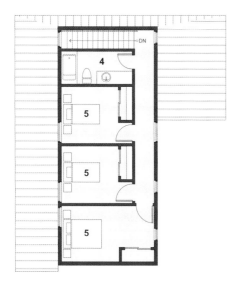

Second Floor

Ground Floor

Key

1 - Living
2 - Dining
3 - Kitchen
4 - Bath
5 - Bedroom
6 - Porch
7 - Courtyard
8 - Rainwater Cistern

1'   5'   10'   20'

view of interior courtyard and cistern

plastering wood-fiber cement block wall

view of houses from street

Chapter 13

Kinsell Commons at Tassafaronga Village

Oakland, California

David Baker and Partners Architects and Habitat for Humanity® East Bay (CA)

Key Partnerships

David Baker, principal with David Baker and Partners Architects (DBPA)

Daniel Simons, principal with David Baker and Partners Architects (DBPA)

Mark Hogan, architect with David Baker and Partners Architects (DBPA)

Natalie Monk, assistant project manager, Habitat for Humanity East Bay (HFHEB)

The Oakland Housing Authority (OHA), City of Oakland, California

Program Summary

Two 2-bedroom, 1.5-bath attached units

1,100 square feet

Sixteen 3-bedroom, 1.5-bath attached units

1,250 square feet

Four 3-bedroom, 2-bath attached units

1,270 square feet

Project Timeline

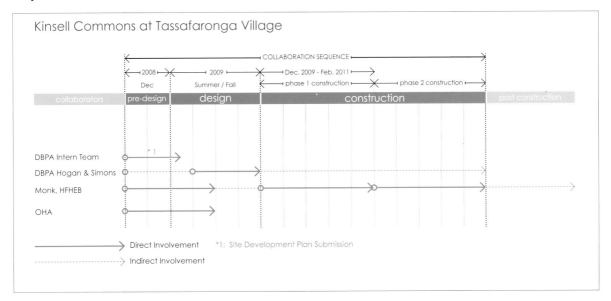

Catalysts for Collaboration

In 2007 the Oakland Housing Authority (OHA) made plans to demolish the Tassafaronga Housing Project, a "severely distressed" public housing project located in East Oakland, and to redevelop the property under the guidelines of the Department of Housing and Urban Development's HOPE VI program, which required a blend of market-rate and affordable units. As part of the redevelopment plan the OHA donated a little more than one acre of the seven-and-a-half-acre site to Habitat for Humanity East Bay (HFHEB): enough land to build twenty-two homes. The target population for the Habitat homes would be displaced former Tassafaronga residents and local renters.[1] As the OHA's plans for redevelopment moved forward, a competitive selection process was conducted to select the designers of the new Tassafaronga Village.

David Baker and Partners Architects (DBPA) of San Francisco was selected to design the project, which called for the redesign of the entire site, including 180 rental housing units, a neighborhood recreation and community center, a playground, pocket parks and open spaces, and pedestrian pathways that connect Tassafaronga Village to the surrounding residential neighborhoods and to one of the few public parks in the area.

Design Process

At the outset of the project DBPA and the OHA determined that the project would be registered in the US Green Building Council's LEED® Neighborhood Development Pilot Project (LEED ND) and that the design team would aim for LEED for Homes certification on all of the Tassafaronga Village units. To be sure that the overall site development plan would meet the requirements of LEED ND certification, which measures sustainable site development strategies at the scale of the entire site, the sites for the twenty-two HFHEB homes needed to be identified early. Consequently, DBPA became involved in discussions with members of HFHEB in the early stages of the Tassafaronga design process. As David Baker recalls, "rather than make that decision in a vacuum, it seemed logical to start talking to Habitat about what size parcels and what kind of units [they planned to build]."

Over the course of several working sessions, DBPA, OHA, and HFHEB developed a site strategy that split the Habitat homes into two parcels, a fourteen-home site on 84th Avenue, and an eight-home site on 81st Avenue. The decision to create two parcels was influenced by a number of factors. The first related to the affiliate's building capacity. As Baker recalls, "Habitat didn't want to build twenty-two units at one time; they only wanted a maximum of twelve to fifteen units under construction at once."

This decision allowed the Habitat homes to be interlaced with the rest of the development rather than concentrated in one area. The two sites, which would be called "Kinsell Commons at Tassafaronga Village," would be integrated into the green pathways and open spaces DBPA was planning for the overall development. The fourteen homes in the first parcel on 84th Avenue would be configured into a combination of "townhouses," consisting of four duplex and two triplex configurations. The eight townhouses on the 81st Avenue parcel would be configured into one duplex and two triplex townhomes.

Baker gave the assignment to develop a schematic design for the Kinsell Commons parcels to a team of intern architects working in their office. With support from HFHEB leadership, the team developed a schematic site plan for both Kinsell Commons parcels, along with a conceptual design for the multi-unit townhomes, allowing the Kinsell Commons parcels to be included in the approved subdivision plan for the overall Tassafaronga Village site.

In late 2008, as DBPA prepared the Tassafaronga Village site plan and the non-Habitat housing units for permit reviews and approvals from the OHA and the City of Oakland, HFHEB decided that it would be essential to have the Kinsell Commons sites share site design and architectural language with the surrounding Tassafaronga buildings. As Natalie Monk, assistant project manager for HFHEB, recalls, "we wanted to make our homes fit in with the rest of Tassafaronga Village and we thought the best way to do that would be by hiring the same architect." DBPA responded by agreeing to do the conceptual design work pro bono.

About a year later, as Tassafaronga Village was nearing the start of construction, HFHEB asked DBPA to develop design and construction documents for the homes in Kinsell Commons. DBPA agreed, with Mark Hogan and Daniel Simons taking the lead roles on the design team. Natalie Monk assumed the lead role for HFHEB.

Hogan and Simons began a series of discussions with staff from HFHEB aimed at understanding the affiliate's design and construction standards. According to Monk, HFHEB was working toward a more integrated design and construction process for its projects, and had recently compiled a set of written design guidelines, which was shared with Hogan and Simons. The design guidelines identified the affiliate's area requirements and specific volunteer-centered construction methods HFHEB prefers to use.

Throughout design development, the design of the site plan stayed essentially the same. Each house had its own backyard, along with access to a shared car court and common green space. Each of the two parcels remained connected to the rest of the Tassafaronga Village via pathways and sidewalks.

The design of the townhome units received the most attention by Simons and Hogan. As the architects recollect, the Kinsell Commons design team and HFHEB project management and construction staff collaborated to carefully tune the design of the townhomes to something that could be built by the volunteers, what Hogan describes as "a process of simplification."

The final scheme for the townhomes featured open floor plans on the ground floor to allow for views of the street and the rear yard, with bedrooms on the second floor. As Hogan recalls, Monk and the HFHEB staff were "very involved with the design process," especially with regard to monitoring projected construction cost and "holding the design team to the target floor areas." HFHEB staff carefully reviewed the drawings at every stage of the process.

Construction Process

The 84th Avenue site broke ground in December 2009, and construction lasted for just over one year. In preparation for construction, HFHEB had a digital model of the framing for the project made so they could see the exact location of every piece of wood that would go in the house in three dimensions. The framing drawings were put to use over the course of the construction phase and during the annual Earth Day Build-A-Thon. The four-day event in 2010 organized the efforts of 750 volunteers in the construction (framing) of ten of the phase 1 homes.

The utilization of "accelerated construction" events or "blitz builds" requires significant pre-construction planning, yet, according to Monk, the events allow the affiliate to accomplish in four days what would normally take several months.

In coordination with the LEED ND certification goals of the overall Tassafaronga development, HFHEB will secure LEED for Homes certification on one of each townhome type, for a total of three homes. Every home will be GreenPoint® rated and Energy Star certified.

In keeping with their green building efforts, HFHEB partners with GRID Alternatives, a local non-profit that installs photovoltaic panels on all new HFHEB homes using volunteer labor. Consequently, every Kinsell Commons home utilizes this technology. The homes are 35 percent more energy efficient than required by California code and, in addition to the panels, are designed to utilize extra insulation and efficient wood framing, thus reducing waste and thermal bridging.

Kinsell Commons also features drought-tolerant plants, high-efficiency irrigation systems, and stormwater systems that filter stormwater through the soil before going to the storm drain system.

Lessons Learned

Hogan and Simons found the HFHEB guidelines to be very useful in terms of initiating and guiding the discussion that the team would have over the several months of the design process. For Simons, however, reviewing past HFHEB projects was also valuable to the design team. "Seeing some of the stuff that they had built was more useful in terms of figuring out what we were actually going to design," he said.

Simons also notes that the involvement of the experienced construction staff from HFHEB was a critical resource to the design team. "Having people who had been through the process multiple times, that knew what they were doing, and that you could talk to about the things that you were working on was great," he said.

As Monk notes, this has become a standard approach for HFHEB, which works with architects on most of its projects. "Our affiliate is very involved with the design process; we review every set of drawings very thoroughly. In part from a construction perspective, in part from knowledge of what our homebuyers want to see, and also for general architectural preferences and desires," said Monk.

Baker echoes the perspective that HFHEB's intensive involvement in the design process was instrumental in the success of the project. Though this process was time consuming for both DBPA and the affiliate, as Baker notes, it was time well invested. "[HFHEB] took a long time to review drawings and get back to us. We spent a long time figuring out what our response was going to be. Each one of those steps takes a really long time," said Baker. The commitment to "not trying to go too fast" allowed the teams to avoid misunderstanding the other's priorities and the nuances of their organizations' mode of work. Adds Baker, "it's better because you figure stuff out."

84th Street site plan (phase 1)

Key

1 - 2 Bedroom Duplex Unit   4 - 3 Bedroom Triplex Unit
2 - 3 Bedroom Duplex Unit   5 - Car Court
3 - 3 Bedroom Accessible Unit   6 - Community Space

10'   30'   60'

aerial view of phase 1 townhomes

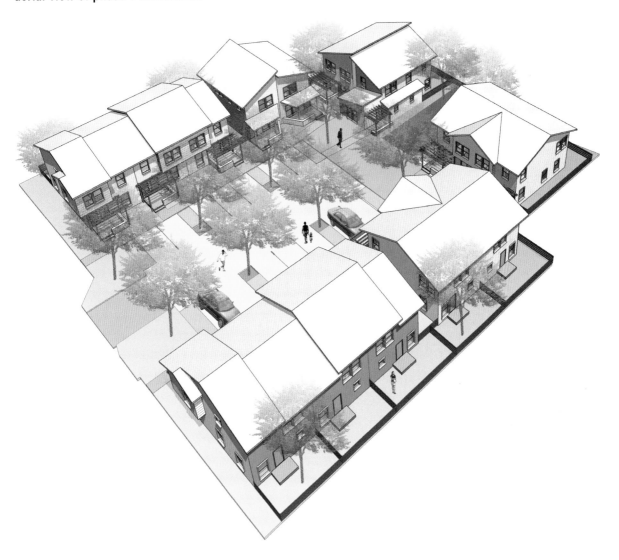

typical three-bedroom unit floor plan

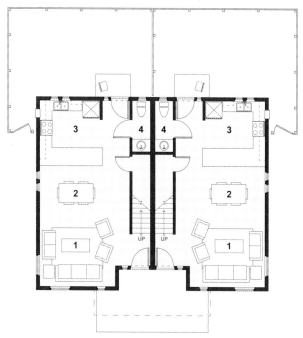

Ground Floor

Second Floor

Key

1 - Living   **4** - Half Bath
2 - Dining   **5** - Bath
3 - Kitchen   **6** - Bedroom

view of unit entry from car court

view of common area

view of phase 1 townhomes

LESSONS FROM THE FIELD

Keys to Making Collaborations Work

David Hinson and Justin Miller

The efforts of the design teams and their Habitat partners profiled in the thirteen cases presented in *Designed for Habitat* offer up a range of valuable lessons for how to make collaborations between architects and Habitat affiliates succeed. Reflecting on the insights we have gained from studying these cases, we find a number of important considerations that should guide architects and their Habitat partners when planning similar collaborations.

As outlined in the preface, among the most important factors contributing to the success of these projects is the ability of the project partners to find a core of common goals around which they could structure their collaboration. Finding this common ground does not come easily.

As we encountered in our own discussions with Habitat founder Millard Fuller, and Rural Studio founder Samuel Mockbee, a shared goal to help low-income families is not likely to be enough to make these partnerships work. It is critical that design teams and their clients are candid and honest about the goals they bring to these partnerships. Unexamined presumptions (by either side) that the goals of the project are clear and compatible can unravel the most well-intentioned efforts to work together.

As John Cary points out in *The Power of Pro Bono*, "The most successful partnerships [between architects and non-profit clients] … rely on a high level of feedback and co-education."[1] In writing about the keys to successful negotiation and collaboration in design practice, Ava Abramowitz notes that the effort to reach common ground regarding goals and motivations has to begin at the very start of projects. She calls this process the "front-end alignment" of the project team, or more specifically, the "alignment of the project participants as to their objectives and ability to work effectively together at the outset of the project."[2]

Understanding Goals and Motivations

In almost every case studied here there was a significant realm of shared goals that bound the participants together and anchored their collaborations. However, even in these successful examples, the partners each brought unique goals and concerns to the table. Before we look at the common ground, we believe it is valuable to look at some of the unique motivations that design teams and their Habitat partners may bring to these ventures.

Design Team Motivations

Though values regarding design and design process will be familiar to readers from the design disciplines, they might not be obvious to Habitat leaders and other would-be partners in the affordable-housing community. The first of these motivations we found marbled through our conversations with the architects interviewed for *Designed for Habitat* is the simple, but strongly held, belief that experienced designers can make Habitat homes better places to live.

The Power of Design

As John Peterson, founder of Public Architecture, explains in *The Power of Pro Bono*, one of the central tenets of the value system shared by most architects is the belief that "well-designed environments can have a profound impact on our lives."[3] Though it would be misguided to suggest that this is the sole motivator of architects in this context, the "master value" status architects assign to the power of good design is at the heart of what draws architects to affordable-housing design efforts—they believe they can make a valuable and meaningful contribution by applying their special skills and talents.[4] The architects and architecture students involved in our case study projects are drawn to the opportunity to put this belief into action.

The design teams we studied consistently expressed the view that the standard design templates utilized by many Habitat affiliates could be "made better" with their help. For many the professional challenge of developing design solutions which (in the designer's eyes) address the shortcomings of the standard designs found in Habitat portfolios is a major motivation in its own right.

The definitions of "better" expressed by the design teams range pretty broadly, but the following perspectives surfaced with the most frequency.

A recurring theme in discussions with design teams was the perception that design quality was not particularly high on the long list of concerns and challenges faced by Habitat affiliate leaders, nor do the architects expect it to be. As our interview with David Baker illustrates, the designers attribute this to the fact that affiliates are focused on many other challenges, such as the challenge of managing costs and organizing construction crews of constantly variable ability. In Baker's view, it is understandable that affiliate staffs are "very pragmatically focused," but consequently, Baker observes, "design is a weakness in Habitat's culture."

This focus on "the pragmatic" aspects of leading a Habitat affiliate is understandable, but from the perspective we have gained from these cases it can also be limiting in ways affiliates might not recognize. As we have seen in several cases, the "pragmatic filters" that emphasize controlling costs and managing unskilled volunteers tends to lead to a decision framework regarding design that is incremental and fragmented. Homes that result from the accumulation of experience-based lessons do not always add up to well-designed homes. Describing her view of how design is framed within the culture of Habitat affiliates, Natalie Monk (HFHEB) recounts, "design decisions impacting the livability of the space or the performance of the site are approached pragmatically, through the keyhole of cost and build-ability. These often result in aggregations of earnest decisions made in absence of a clear picture of the implications of one decision upon the next." As the descriptions of the design process in the cases profiled here illustrate, a consistent element of a professional design team's approach is the effort to integrate responses to separate aspects of the design problem into an "integrated whole" solution.

Customization versus Standardization

Architects are trained that the path to good design solutions begins with a clear understanding of end user's needs; the more specific and nuanced the better. Additionally, architects are trained to study individual sites and respond to the specific conditions of the site through the design process. As Mooney and Posada observe, "to have a really affordable sustainable home, you really have to understand the nuances of the site, and it really has to respond to those specific site conditions. This is a challenge with Habitat sometimes, because they are building so many houses in so many places. It's hard to take every single one and make it specific to wherever that site may be."

The dialogue regarding sustainability and green design has begun to open up the issue of attention to site-specific design responses, as affiliates

the layout of porches, storage, and interior circulation for the DESIGNhabitat 3.1 home is designed to change based on the solar orientation of the site (Chapter 4)

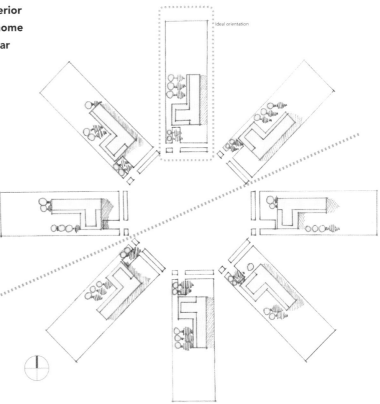

become more aware of the relationship between solar exposure and energy use.

By far the most frequently cited conflict regarding design we heard was over the limited role of Habitat homeowner families in the design process. Over the course of our conversations with the design teams it was clear that the architects felt they could be most effective when they could have direct access to, and interaction with, the family that would own the home they were designing. As Rick Sundberg notes, "When I have a client who is really involved with design, I think I do my best work and the best projects come out of it."

Though most of the architects we interviewed for *Designed for Habitat* were reconciled to the limited access to homeowners stipulated by their affiliate partners, they point out that feedback from end users can also have the benefit of helping designers filter out ideas that seem good in the abstract, but do not mesh with the perceptions or needs of end user families.

Citing the example of the exposed, stained-concrete floors in the Webster Street homes,

design team meeting with Habitat families to gather design input for Project 1800 (Chapter 7)

Mooney and Posada note, "I think it's important for people with our level of experience to recognize that the things that young architects get excited about are not always the same things that homeowners get excited about."

The flip side of this ethos is to view standardized plans as less valuable, or, more specifically, less likely to realize the quality of life enhancements that architects believe they bring to the design of affordable housing. John Peterson echoes this belief, asserting that, "If the design does not respond to the particular needs of a community, it isn't good design."[5]

Though many professional architects have learned that affordable housing is generally not delivered via individually customized home designs, the belief that standard templates are inherently less valuable than customized solutions is deeply ingrained in their professional ethos.

As noted in the preface and illustrated in many of the cases we have profiled, the issue of how much the home design will be tailored to the homeowner client can be a major source of tension in partnerships between architects and Habitat affiliates. As seen in the VPH House project, this tension can be particularly challenging to manage when partnering with architecture schools. In these cases, the faculty directing the projects has a responsibility to teach their students the skills and methods professional architects employ when working with clients, and they see these community-based projects as a perfect opportunity to "learn by doing."

professional "super jury" members reviewing student design proposals for DESIGNhabitat 2 (Chapter 1)

Successful partnerships between architects and their Habitat partners will require early agreement regarding the degree of homeowner interaction that the design team will have, and the level of customization that will be pursued in their process.

Making Small Homes that "Live Large"

Understanding that highly-customized solutions are problematic for affiliates, the design teams profiled in *Designed for Habitat* most often sought to compensate for limited access to homeowners by developing design solutions that would allow families greater flexibility in the ways they used interior spaces, in particular what the architects referred to as the "social spaces" of the home—the living and dining spaces and the kitchen. Though the layout of bedrooms and baths in houses profiled in *Designed for Habitat* tends to emphasize compact and efficient configurations, the designs favor open, flexible

plan configurations for the social spaces. As was the case in the Stiles Street homes, the plans often allow homeowners the option of assigning the living and dining activities to interchangeable spaces, depending on the family's preference for locating these spaces on the front or rear of the home.

This goal is echoed in the way Chuck Roberts describes the design for the Stanley Street homes. "We wanted to create a house that felt like it had an open plan. These houses are very small. If you start to cut up living rooms, dining rooms, and kitchens you just end up with a bunch of little spaces. So we definitely wanted to have the kitchen, living, and dining feel like one open space, which they do," said Roberts.

The design teams also place an emphasis on utilizing taller room volumes (via double-height spaces and vaulted ceilings) in the social spaces and the use of natural light and views through the

cross-section through DESIGNhabitat 2 home (Chapter 1)

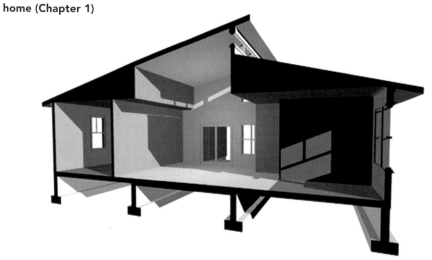

view of vaulted ceiling in central space of the DESIGNhabitat 2 home (Chapter 1)

view of vaulted kitchen and dining area in the habiTECH09 home (Chapter 5)

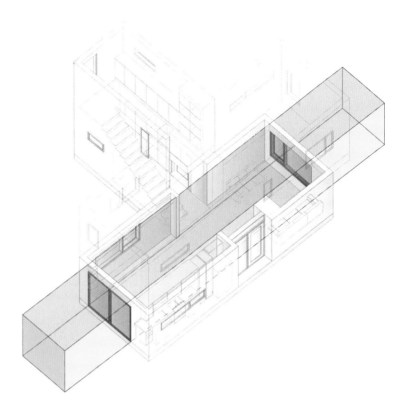

house to the site beyond as a means of making the homes feel "brighter and more airy." This strategy was employed in the DESIGNhabitat 2 house, Habitat Trails, ecoMOD4, habiTECH09, Roxbury Estates, and several others. As Roberts explained, the Stanley Street design team consciously sought to design specific "view experiences" as they composed homes. "We liked the idea of coming in the front door and seeing that view down through that main volume and seeing the views to the south. … Those [design strategies] were a natural evolution of the open plan, the site orientation of the house, and the way light came in," explained Roberts.

As Quale notes, the student design team for the ecoMOD4 project pursued similar goals. He reports that the students nicknamed the design "Thru House" due to the emphasis they placed on open views and cross-ventilation.

Another common strategy was the integration of exterior living spaces (such as porches or courtyards) in such a way as to "make the small homes live larger." In the case of the DESIGNhabitat 2 home, the large screen porch on the front of the home was proportioned as a room rather than a shallow add-on, allowing the family an "extra room" to eat and gather.

**site plan for Roxbury Estates showing varied
layers of exterior spaces (Chapter 8)**

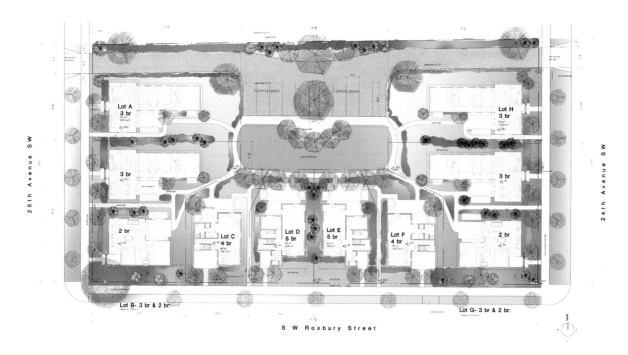

Several project teams configured their plans around specific exterior spaces, such as the shared courtyard in the Webster Street homes and the common car courts and community gardens in Project 1800, Roxbury Estates, and Kinsell Commons. Rick Sundberg describes this as an intentional effort to provide homeowners with a range of shared and private spaces (what Sundberg described as "layers of outdoor space") to choose from. "We tried to take a small project like that and [give homeowners] a bigger backyard communal space and then a smaller, semi-private back porch area," explains Sundberg.

Designing Homes with "Character"

A recurring theme in our discussions with the design teams interviewed for *Designed for Habitat* is the belief that the homeowner families they are designing for deserve homes that reflect the same attention to design as they would provide for paying clients. John Cary describes this as a motivation to design "spaces which go beyond the bare minimum of their intended purpose to become places that foster a sense of belonging and dignity."[6] Echoing Cary's terms, "giving the homes more dignity" was the most frequently used way our design teams define this goal.

The way this goal is pursued by the design teams profiled here is very broad, including several solutions designed to relate more directly to the appearance of their surrounding neighbors, thus mitigating the stigma of "looking like low-income housing," and integrating Habitat families more seamlessly into neighborhoods of mixed economic means. Other design teams have sought to imbue their homes with a unique design character, expressing the belief that low-income families they are designing for deserve the highest level of creativity they can provide, comparable to what they would do for the most well-off client.

Rick Sundberg describes the challenge of designing affordable houses versus homes for affluent clients this way: "I think it's about editing. We have clients that let us explore amazing detail and ideas sometimes. I still bring all those aspirations to a project like this, but … edit it down. We want [our affordable homes] to be good pieces of architecture, something that stands next to anything else we've done."

Though many of the Habitat affiliate leaders we spoke with viewed these objectives favorably, their main reservations were (understandably) the cost implications associated with these goals. In most cases, we found the design teams eagerly embraced the challenge of designing to meet the budget constraints of their affiliate partners, and they believed their design aspirations and the affiliates' concerns could be reconciled. Though the projects that served as special "test cases" regarding new technologies and construction systems

view of Roxbury Estates homes illustrating attention to detail and scale on exterior of the homes (Chapter 8)

were the exception, many of the projects profiled here were built at costs comparable to what the affiliates report as their norm.

Ironically, a few cases in *Designed for Habitat* also illustrate that efforts by design teams to imbue their Habitat homes with character and quality—even when accomplished at comparable cost to standard Habitat homes—can still encounter the perception that the homes "look too nice." As noted in the preface, the view that affordable housing should look different than market-rate housing has deep roots in our culture.[7] It's not likely to go away anytime soon.

Academic Design Team Goals

The academic collaborations bring all of the issues outlined above to the table, along with a few unique ones related to the teaching mission of the architecture program. Many of these goals pose little conflict for affiliates and are, as reported to us, among the most satisfying elements of these collaborations. These include the desire to have students understand the complex design and cost issues associated with the affordable-housing sector, the relationship between design strategies and building performance, learning how creative teams craft successful collaborations (with each other and with their clients and project partners), and understanding the relationship between design and construction via hands-on involvement in the construction process (that is "the design/build experience"). In every academic collaboration case we studied, the affiliate leaders cited the energy, enthusiasm, and commitment of the students they worked with as one of the most positive and satisfying aspects of the partnership.

As noted earlier, the biggest source of tension between academic design teams and their Habitat partners is the degree of access the students will have to the homeowner, and the degree of customized, one-of-a-kind character the design team will be allowed to pursue. In the case of the VPH House, the faculty/student team had to "push hard" to be allowed access to the homeowner family, reports David Baird. In contrast, Kevin Stevens and his Habitat partner Allen Tuten seem to accept the student/homeowner interaction without much tension or conflict.

Failure to reach agreement on the latitude afforded students regarding design character of the home can leave both sides of the partnership smarting from the conflict, as illustrated by the frustration expressed by Baird when his affiliate partner removed the Polygal™ walls, a key design feature of the home, after the home was complete.

Affiliates with longer records of collaboration with architecture schools, such as with the habiTECH partnership, also seem to take the exuberance of the students' design ambitions in stride. As Tuten notes, "While [the habiTECH 09 house] may not be the appearance of a home that I would choose, I have to look at a broader purpose there. The houses are extremely well built and the houses are very comfortable and

architecture students constructing the DESIGNhabitat 2 home (Chapter 1)

view of Polygal walls on VPH home (Chapter 3)

livable. The students have tried to take into consideration future maintenance, utility costs, and green space around the houses. They have been very conscientious."

The unique design solutions arising from student efforts can have other, unexpected consequences. As Pam Dorr notes regarding the DESIGNhabitat 2 home, the house has drawn positive and welcomed attention. "The thing we were most surprised about was how many people travel here to see that house," she notes, adding that the special character of the project helped jumpstart the efforts to get her fledgling affiliate started, and attracted an influx of new partners and volunteers.

Affiliate Goals and Motivations

As we will address in the sections below, in many cases the affiliates we studied in *Designed for Habitat* sought assistance from their architect partners because conditions tied to the project site prevented them from utilizing their more standard approach.

When this motivation was *not* the driving consideration, we found that the key factor in the success of the projects was the position of the project in the affiliate's overall view of its strategic goals and mission. In most of the successful cases, the affiliate leadership had a clear view of how the project fit in their overall strategic plan, and how that context shaped their position regarding the design latitude afforded the design team.

In the example of DESIGNhabitat 2, eco-MOD4, and the Webster Street collaborations, the affiliates viewed these as "demonstration projects"—outside what they would replicate, but valuable as projects that would push forward their understanding of sustainable design and energy conservation. Recognizing these projects would encounter unique costs associated with the special construction systems and technologies involved, the affiliate (and the design teams in some cases) made sure that supplemental funding was in place to cover the differential cost of these projects.

Even in settings where the goals are focused on exploring new approaches, it is important that the scope of the "investigation" is well defined. In the case of Habitat Trails, the "demonstration project perspective" framed the site design aspect of the project for HFHBC, and by all accounts this aspect of the project was a resounding success. However, this perspective did not extend to the affiliate's view of the home designs developed by the UA Community Design Center team. Failure to communicate the shift in perspective associated with these two components of the project brought a great deal of stress to the partnership.

Other affiliates seemed willing to tolerate a pretty broad range of design, as long as the home was well constructed. In the end, Tuten adds, partnership between his affiliate and the habiTECH students provides "an opportunity for another family to get a home built that otherwise would not have one."

Designing for "Volunteer-Friendly" Construction

Even though they were conscious of the issue, many of the design teams we interviewed admitted to underestimating the implications of Habitat's commitment to building with unskilled community volunteers. As Carmen Schleiger points out, "a designer thinking about how to put together a [Habitat] house needs to understand what a Habitat site supervisor deals with every day: a new construction crew—and no idea of their capabilities."

Building with unskilled construction teams means that the "little things get magnified," explains Schleiger, which often leads affiliates to rely upon proven means and methods to the exclusion of alternative approaches, even when they believe those alternatives might result in better homes, or faster and more efficient construction. As Schleiger notes, "in order for us to really achieve the quality goals that we have, our construction needs to be really, really simple," both in terms of design and construction. As with the example of the New Columbia Villa project, this emphasis on "simplification" surfaced again, and again, as the design teams described the pre-construction "editing" sessions they had with their affiliate partners.

Common Ground

Examining the "catalysts for collaboration" in the thirteen case studies in *Designed for Habitat* provides three major issues that brought the Habitat affiliates and their design partners together and served as the critical basis for their partnership. In most cases, at least two of these goals shaped the project.

Partnerships convened to address a specific project context challenge

Almost every Habitat affiliate leader we have met has reported the experience of encountering resistance to the construction of Habitat homes when they propose to build within established neighborhoods. The origins of this community resistance come from many complex sources, both social and aesthetic. Regardless of true origins, the objections often center on the visual contrast between Habitat homes and the character of existing homes in the community. As addressed in the preface, Habitat affiliates have a broad range of positions regarding concessions to local design standards, but several of the cases profiled in *Designed for Habitat* offer examples worth emulating for affiliates inclined towards the "community partnership" position.[8]

Projects such as New Columbia Villa, Project 1800, Stiles Street, and Stanley Street provide examples of homes that had to be designed to integrate with a specific community context—often with an external approval required. Each provides a successful example of a design solution that responds to both community context and Habitat's core values.

view of new Stiles Street homes (center) with typical homes found in the neighborhood on left. The affiliate's first home built in the neighborhood is on the far right (Chapter 9)

Demonstrating success in these community integration projects can have valuable post-project benefits for affiliates. As recounted by M.J. Adams, the success of the Stanley Street project strengthened the affiliate's credibility within the local development community and brought them new partners and new home sites.

These projects also illustrate the careful balancing act that design teams and their affiliate partners face when trying to reconcile accommodations to community context and the project budgeting and volunteer-centered construction process standards of the affiliate. Though the New Columbia Villa homes managed to accommodate community context accommodations with little impact on cost, concessions made to community groups on the Stiles Street homes pushed the Philadelphia affiliate past the point they believed was sustainable regarding home size and cost.

Partnerships convened to explore new construction approaches and technologies

Many of the cases feature initiatives aimed at evaluating construction approaches and technologies that are unfamiliar to the affiliate, but nevertheless offer the promise of addressing an important problem. This objective is illustrated by the exploration of modular production approaches explored in the DESIGNhabitat 2 and ecoMOD4 projects, the experiments with prefabrication on Project 1800 and DESIGNhabitat 3, and the multiple examples where teams used projects to explore approaches to construction systems such as insulated concrete

prefabricated module for DESIGNhabitat 2.1 home being lifted on to foundation (Chapter 1)

formwork (ICF) and Structural Insulated Panel System (SIPS).

As with the community context issue, incorporating these non-standard construction technologies requires a careful approach to managing the associated costs, and to managing expectations regarding the role of unskilled volunteers in the construction process. In the most successful cases, such as the Webster Street homes, the new systems were constructed by an experienced

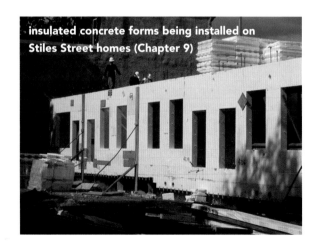

insulated concrete forms being installed on Stiles Street homes (Chapter 9)

professional team (or a team of students prepared by extensive research), and then evaluated relative to their "volunteer friendliness." Examples where this level of support was not present, such as with the SIPS used on the first home at Habitat Trails, illustrate how difficult handling these unfamiliar systems (and their design implications) can be for affiliates.

As noted earlier, the additional costs associated with using new systems are occasionally embedded in "hidden" labor costs. This is illustrated by the DESIGNhabitat 2 home, where labor costs were embedded in the factory-based construction of the modules. This premium was anticipated, and the team secured support from a private foundation to address the differential associated with the modular approach.

Partnerships convened to advance sustainable design and construction goals

Sustainability, and more specifically lower energy cost for homeowners, seems to offer the most encouraging "common ground" of all the major catalysts for collaboration we encountered in these cases. The objective of "building green" connects to a set of compelling professional values regarding architects' ethical duties to integrate sustainable-design principles into their work (a value shared by many affiliate leaders) and, as noted in the preface, it connects directly to Habitat's motivation to provide financial security for their client families.

As the cases profiled here illustrate, the goal of building more sustainable homes makes it essential for affiliates to think holistically about project design, that is to consider how all aspects of the design work together to contribute to more sustainable solutions—from building orientation to window specification. As noted earlier, this way of thinking about design is embedded in the way architects are trained, making their assistance particularly valuable to Habitat affiliates.

Sustainable design objectives played a significant role in almost every case studied in *Designed for Habitat*. For some teams this goal was pursued via simple modifications to construction standards, such as better insulation strategies and more efficient mechanical equipment—what Paul McKean of the New Columbia Villa design team called "the low-hanging fruit of green design." For other teams, as with the Webster Street homes, the designs included ambitious "investigations" with new systems and innovative technologies.

The benefits of this focus on energy conservation are tangible and easy to understand for both design teams and their affiliate partners. As the students involved in the DESIGNhabitat 3 project came to understand, low-income families spend a higher percentage of their income on energy bills (as much as 33 percent in Alabama) than do more affluent families.

The results of the energy conservation strategies employed in our case study projects are impressive in this regard. As John Musselman of HFHP noted, the energy conservation features of the Stiles Street homes have resulted in 75 percent lower energy bills than customary on other HFHP homes. The

graph of HERS rating improvements resulting from redesign of DESIGNhabitat 3 homes in response to energy modeling studies (Chapter 4)

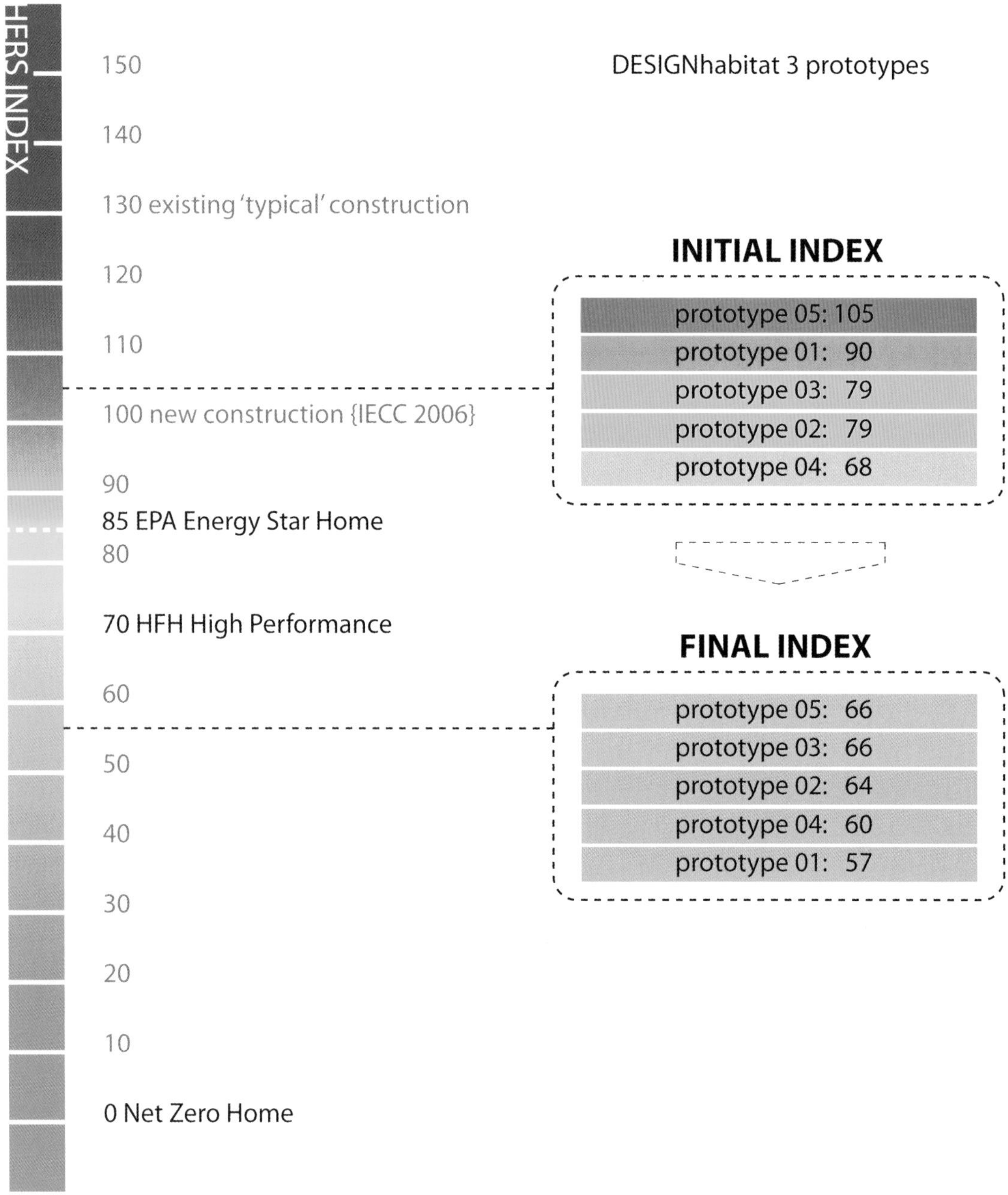

HERS INDEX

150	DESIGNhabitat 3 prototypes
140	
130 existing 'typical' construction	
120	
110	
100 new construction {IECC 2006}	
90	
85 EPA Energy Star Home	
80	
70 HFH High Performance	
60	
50	
40	
30	
20	
10	
0 Net Zero Home	

INITIAL INDEX

prototype 05: 105
prototype 01:   90
prototype 03:   79
prototype 02:   79
prototype 04:   68

FINAL INDEX

prototype 05: 66
prototype 03: 66
prototype 02: 64
prototype 04: 60
prototype 01: 57

Stanley Street homes have also surprised the affiliate with the impact of the design on energy savings. The 2.5 kilowatt photovoltaic panels used on the first Stanley Street home often produce more electricity than the super-insulated home needs. Since the surplus automatically returns to the electric grid, notes M.J. Adams, "The homeowner reports that on several occasions her monthly statement has shown a credit balance of as much as $80."

Some partnerships utilize their collaborations to explore the compatibility of third-party certification programs (such as Energy Star, LEED® for Homes, and so on) with the affiliate's goals for their projects. As Messinetti recalls, "just going through the LEED process was a learning experience—because we had so many experts at the table with us: the Cascadia Green Building Council, Green Hammer (LEED consultants), the designers and so forth. Working through that we learned a lot about LEED certification, how to get there."

Though we have not surveyed affiliates beyond our thirteen case study projects, LEED certification seems valuable for its design and construction principles, but burdensome in its documentation requirements. Many of the affiliates we interviewed report that they will try to build to LEED standards—seeing the value that these standards bring to their project—but few will opt to pursue actual LEED certification of their buildings unless that is a specific requirement of the context for the project (such as with Kinsell Commons). As in the case of the Portland affiliate, which now has several LEED-certified projects to its credit, some affiliates are choosing to utilize third-party certifications that are less time intensive to complete, such as the EarthCraft Homes and Earth Advantage® Home programs.

In many cases, the innovations advocated by the design teams served to help affiliates make significant advances in the standards they use on all their homes. As in the example of the Stiles Street homes, the lessons learned from the collaborations with professional design teams have a long-lasting impact. Several of the affiliates we interviewed echoed the sentiment of Frank Monaghan of HFHP, who told us "we would not be where we are with green design today without WRT."

Best-Practice Communication Strategies

In addition to their success at finding common ground to anchor their partnerships, we found many examples where communication challenges presented obstacles for the architects and their Habitat partners, and many examples of creative and effective solutions to these challenges.

Pre-construction Communications

In every successful case we studied, there was an extensive amount of communication (and negotiation) between the affiliate, the design team, and other key stakeholders during the design phase of the project.

As John Quale observed, these sessions involved a healthy mix of design review and critique from the affiliate, along with "detailed discussions regarding schedule and budget control." Though this process inevitably requires "lots and lots of meetings," notes Quale, it is an essential component of the means by which the partners establish trust and confidence in each other.

In every case where it was a part of the project process, the time devoted to pre-construction analysis and review by affiliate representatives and other partners experienced with construction was valued by the design team. In almost every case where this review process was skipped or abbreviated, problems surfaced once the construction phase began.

As with the examples of the Webster Street and Stanley Street projects, many design teams expressed the view that their design solutions improved via this rigorous review process. As Scott Mooney and David Posada note, the process of working with the representative from the affiliate and the construction firm slated to build the home helped them distill the design down to a "cleaner" solution, stripped of "the extra gear and extra stuff" that may have been left in without the collaborative effort to simplify the design.

The teams also stressed that success comes from a commitment to giving the process adequate time to evolve, "not trying to rush through this stage of the process." As David Simons of the Kinsell Commons team observed, "it really comes down to regular meetings, because a lot of this stuff is the stuff that kind of trickles out." David Baker echoes Simons' view, adding that the multiple cycles of review and response they experienced gave the design teams and their affiliate partner the time "to figure stuff out."

The nature of design practice, where every project is a customized solution, makes the intensity of interaction in this phase familiar to architects. Affiliates, particularly those that most commonly build from standard design templates (provided by HFHI or other sources), are often less prepared to commit the requisite attention of their key leadership during this phase. As noted at the beginning of this chapter, this point in the process is *the* place where communication regarding goals and expectations is most critical.

The design phase input can be especially challenging in academic collaborations, as the project schedule is constrained by the academic calendar. In these instances, affiliates and their faculty partners have to make special provisions in their schedules to ensure this pre-construction review and feedback stage is not bypassed.

As the testimonials from the cases we've studied here attest, it is important for both design teams and affiliate leadership to understand that these collaborations require affiliates to commit the time and focus of their key leadership to this point in the process for these special initiatives to succeed.

In our assessment, problems and conflicts related to budget control, constructability, and design latitude that arise in some of the cases profiled in *Designed for Habitat* can most often be traced back to insufficient communications at this pre-construction stage.

Continuity of Key Leadership

A corollary to the importance of pre-construction

alignment of expectations is the importance of continuity in the key stakeholders. This is certainly the case in the habiTECH program where, as Kevin Stevens recounts, the consistency of the board has allowed a "long-term commitment" to develop. Stevens aligns the work of the habiTECH program with its affiliate partner by staying in close communication with them before, during, and after each round of design and construction. Stevens tries to participate in all of the monthly meetings of the HFHNCL Board of Directors, and begins planning the next round of work with the board during the summer after each house is completed. Though this partnership stands out as an example that would be hard for most to replicate, it illustrates the effort and commitment required to make that sustained partnership work. The six homes completed in the habiTECH program to date are evidence that the strategy works!

We heard of several instances, such as in the VPH House project and Habitat Trails, where a change in the affiliate director or a changeover in the affiliate board, without buy-in on the goals that shape the project from their successors, can erase even the best efforts at "front-end alignment."[9]

In the Habitat Trails example, as Stephen Luoni recounts, the UACDC design team seemed to have broad support from both the staff and the board of the Benton County affiliate throughout the site design and approvals stage. However, a change in the makeup of the board (coinciding with the construction of the first house) seemed to result in a change of attitude—from positive to skeptical—from this key group. David Baird attributes a similar "chill" in his relationship with the Baton Rouge affiliate when the affiliate's executive director (the project's main champion) left her position. Both projects finished with commendable (even award-winning) results, but the relationships were fractured beyond repair.

Documenting Agreements (Early!)

Based on the experience of several rounds of collaborations with community-based non-profit groups, John Quale captures the agreements reached during the planning stages of his projects in a "memorandum of understanding," or MOU. The MOU developed for the ecoMOD4 project addressed the project design goals, how the project budget would be funded and managed, and the division of responsibility between the student team and the affiliate relative to the on-site construction elements of the project. Several teams referenced their use of contracts and other forms of agreements between the design team and the Habitat affiliate, but few seemed to address the key goals as clearly as the MOU described by Quale. By addressing expectations so directly, the MOU provided the team with a critical tool to manage the inevitable changes that arose over the course of the project.

Developing Tools to Support Key Decisions

During the initial design study phase of the Stiles Street project, the project team and the affiliate faced a complex set of decisions regarding the range of design and construction features that would be

**Design Challenge Matrix used on the Stiles Street
homes to prioritize design strategies (Chapter 9)**

Parkside neighborhood context	Habitat 'standard'	Alternative solutions	Compromise
Three-story buildings	Two-story building	Two-story building Three-story building	Two-story building for Habitat units (with three-story façade); three-story for market-rate units
Continuous street façade/row houses	Twins		Row houses
Generous floor-to-floor heights (and resulting window heights)	8 FT to underside ceiling (full sheet of GWB) 1,140 SF for 3 BR unit; 1,200 SF for 4 BR unit		Match existing (Habitat cost premium) Larger units (Habitat cost premium)
Masonry (brick) façades	Siding-type exterior wall material (volunteer labor versus skilled labor)	Brick Stucco Siding	Brick (Habitat cost premium)
Dark-colored façades	Lighter colors (standard vinyl siding)		Use dark colors, if using siding; paint stucco dark color? (side walls)
Continuous porch	Small porch	Continuous porch Individual porch	Continuous porch (Habitat cost premium)
Flat roof with parapet detail	Sloped roof (< 6:12) (installation and insurance impact)	Flat roof Sloped roof	Single-slope roof, with three-story, parapet-type façade for Habitat units; flat roof for market-rate units
No setback from sidewalk	Meet zoning (= 8 FT from street ROW)		0 FT setback from sidewalk (match adjacent buildings)

involved in responding to the surrounding neighborhood context and with achieving the LEED certification goals for the project. To facilitate these choices, Maarten Pesch and his team developed a "Design Challenge Matrix," which presented each element of the proposed design in comparison with the affiliate's standard approach, and explained the impact of each alternative on the overall objectives of LEED certification and neighborhood acceptance of the design. The Design Challenge Matrix helped Musselman and the HFHP board understand how their standard design approach, the goal of neighborhood compatibility, and the goal of LEED certification compared across a broad spectrum of design decisions embedded in the project.

With the new digital tools accessible to designers (and their affiliate partners) comes a whole new set of tools to help affiliates evaluate design options. In the case of the DESIGNhabitat 3 studio, the use of energy analysis software allowed the student design teams to test a range of wall, roof, and floor assemblies, mechanical systems, building orientation, and so on, and quickly see the impact of these choices on the energy demands of the home design. More importantly, the tools allowed them to revise the design until it met AAHA's target goals.

In another example of how new digital tools can facilitate decision making, the Kinsell Commons team used digitally generated 3-D framing models to allow HFHP affiliate leaders to evaluate alternative framing options and understand potential construction phase difficulties. The on-site construction manager was able to utilize this information to more effectively manage the efforts of hundreds of volunteers during "accelerated construction" events.

As these examples highlight, design teams and their affiliate partners need to be as conscious and attuned to the dynamics of their communications as they are to the design objectives of their projects. Attention to both aspects of the process is a key signature of the most successful cases we studied in *Designed for Habitat*.

Conclusion

These thirteen cases provide compelling evidence that architecture students and architects can find common ground between their values and those of their would-be partners in Habitat for Humanity. By working carefully and collaboratively, these teams have produced homes of remarkable quality, and enriched the lives of the families that own them.

In addition to providing ample design inspiration, studying these cases from the view of the process used by the teams to achieve these results provides valuable insights regarding the means by which these inspiring designs came to be.

We hope that reading *Designed for Habitat* will serve to motivate architects and affiliates to reach out and help each other: a "catalyst for collaboration" in its own right, if you will.

As our friend and colleague the late Samuel Mockbee would say, "Proceed and be bold!"

AFTERWORD

Despite the cautionary advice of our professional peers regarding the compatibility of Habitat as a partner, we found that careful and patient work to explore the boundaries of our shared values and goals resulted in fertile ground for the creation of homes that would satisfy our Habitat partners, fulfill our personal and professional goals, and change the lives of our client families. Along the way we developed close friendships with the Habitat leaders and volunteers we worked with and the families we helped.

We found our experience was not unique. As the cases profiled in *Designed for Habitat* attest, though success requires more than a shared desire to help low-income families, partnerships between Habitat and architects can yield homes of inspiring quality and help affiliates become more effective at addressing their core mission of eliminating poverty housing. We hope the results illustrated by *Designed for Habitat* will inspire architects, architecture students, and Habitat leaders to reach out to each other to produce "simple, decent homes" that "shelter the soul." The families we serve deserve no less.

David Hinson   Justin Miller

ACKNOWLEDGMENTS

The geneses for this book were the terrific collaboration experiences we have had with Habitat for Humanity® leaders in Alabama. Chief among our Habitat partners were Karen McCauley, former executive director of the Alabama Association of Habitat Affiliates (AAHA), and Andy Bell, also with AAHA. Their support, and the support provided by the AAHA Board, made the DESIGNhabitat program a success, and led us to seek out other success stories to learn from.

The effort to find those success stories and compile them into Designed for Habitat was supported by the efforts of a team of graduate research assistants from the School of Architecture, Planning, and Landscape Architecture at Auburn: Lauren Havard, Samantha Hitchcock, Evan Jacobsen, Haley Rune, and David Watson. Their efforts were invaluable to this project.

Each case study profiled in Designed for Habitat was developed with the assistance and input of the key project partners involved. We would like to acknowledge the generous contributions of time and project materials provided by each of the following individuals and organizations, and thank them for their time and enthusiasm for this book project. In addition, we wish to acknowledge the contributions of the design teams that made these projects possible:

Chapter 1
DESIGNhabitat 2
The material for this case study was developed from David Hinson's firsthand experience with the project and an interview with Pamela Dorr, executive director of the Habitat for Humanity Hale County affiliate.

Stacy Norman, architect and adjunct faculty member at Auburn University, shared the role of directing the DESIGNhabitat 2 project with Hinson. Students involved in the DESIGNhabitat 2 project included: Joey Aplin, Samuel Bassett, Cayce Bean, David Davis, Danielle Dratch, Joey Fante, Russ Gibbs, Jennifer Givens, Simon Hurst, Walter Mason, Bill Moore, Matt Murphy, Ryan Simon, and Mackenzie Stagg.

Significant assistance on the DESIGNhabitat 2 home was provided by the staff of the Palm Harbor Homes production plant in Boaz, Alabama, particularly Greg Peet.

Students involved in the DESIGNhabitat 2.1 project included: Daniel Ash, Christian Ayala, Samuel Bassett, Allan Harris, Mark Porth, and Michael Shows.

Significant assistance on the DESIGNhabitat 2.1 home was provided by the staff of Nationwide Custom Homes production plant in Arabi, Georgia, particularly Kevin Law.

Chapter 2
Habitat Trails
The material for this case study was developed from interviews with professor Stephen Luoni, director of the University of Arkansas Community Design Center; Debbie Wieneke, executive director of Habitat for Humanity Benton County; and Pat Adams, volunteer and board member with Habitat for Humanity Benton County.

In addition to Luoni, key University of Arkansas faculty and staff involved in the design team included Leslie Bartsch, professor Mark Boyer, Aaron Gabriel, Britt Hill, Jeffrey Huber, Adam Jokerst, Amy Marbury, Dr Marty Matlock, John McWilliams, Isaac Moran, James Meyer, Jennifer Raible, and Roberto Sangalli.

The project design team also received assistance from John Wary and Sammi May, of Morrison Shipley Engineers; and John Mack of JKJ Architects.

Students involved in the Habitat Trails design team included David Anderson, Jared Hueter, Remick Moore, Cari Paulus, Lauren Ratley, Rachel Smith, Matt Snyder, and John Starnes.

Chapter 3
VPH House
The material for this case study was developed from interviews with professor David Baird, former faculty member at the Louisiana State University (currently with the School of Architecture at the University of Las Vegas); Lynn Clark, executive director of Habitat for Humanity Greater Baton Rouge; and Mark Montgomery, volunteer with Habitat for Humanity Greater Baton Rouge.

Students involved in the VPH House project included John Batey, Johnnie Beadle, Hunter Brown, Pasquale De Paola, Zachary Evans, Jonathan Fernandez, Frederick Gauthreaux, Guy Gregorie, Sarah Guthrie, Aleah Hargrave, Ana Hernandez, Carlos Perret, Erica Royalty, Brad Silvia, John Stoker, and Brian Waits.

Assistance was also provided by Judith Nordgren, director of the Vinyl Institute, and George Middleton, architect and consultant for the Vinyl Institute.

Chapter 4
DESIGNhabitat 3
The material for this case study was developed from Justin Miller's firsthand experience with the project and interviews with Andy Bell of the Alabama Association of Habitat Affiliates, and Rusty Miller of Habitat for Humanity Escambia County.

Students involved in the DESIGNhabitat 3 project included Daniel Beeker, Kimberly Edwards, Will Hart, Nicholas Henninger, Lea Henley, Sinae Kim, Courtney Mathias, Nick Paolucci, Mayur Patel, Amanda Petersson, Mark Porth, Michael Shows, David Simons, and T. Scott Smith.

Chapter 5
habiTECH09
The material for this case study was developed from interviews with professor Kevin Stevens from Louisiana Tech University's School of Architecture and Allen Tuten, former executive director and member of the Board of Directors for Habitat for Humanity North Central Louisiana.

Students involved in the habiTECH09 design studio included Jared Boudreaux, Marcus Calhoun, Evan Dowden, Craig Jirak, Dominic Johnson, Lance Matthews, Hoi San Sio, Laura Thomas, and Grant Waggenspack.

Assistance was also provided by Contects: Consultants and Architects, LEED Provider.

Chapter 6
ecoMOD4

The material for this case study was developed from interviews with professor John Quale of the University of Virginia (UVA) School of Architecture, and Dan Rosenweig and Audrey Storm of the Habitat for Humanity Greater Charlottesville affiliate.

Other UVA faculty and staff involved in the ecoMOD4 project included Paxton Marshall, Harry Powell, Ronald Williams, Joanna Curran, and Mike Curry of the School of Engineering and Applied Sciences; and Nancy Takahashi, Eric Field, Jeff Erkelens, and Nisha Botchwey of the School of Architecture. Greg Sloditskie served as a modular building advisor. Jeff Erkelens and Susan Riddle also served as consultants to the project.

Students involved in the ecoMOD4 project included: Emily Anderson, Edric Barnes, Rebekah Berlin, Matt Bowyer, Alex Bragg, Cory Caldwell, Meg Carpenter, Allegra Churchill, Matthew Cleveland, Katie Clinton, Sarah Collins, Lauren DiBianca, Daniele Diner, Bernie Doherty, Kevin Eady, Gregory Ericksen, Larry Galante, Alex Garrison, Andrew Hamm, Hamid Hashime, Ethan Heil, Del Hepler, Kaitlyn Howling, Steven Jackson, Steven Johnson, Jennifer Jones, Matt Jungclaus, Regine Kennedy, John Kupstas, Winnie Lai, Rachel Lau, Yuxun Lei, Suchit Ligade, Zach Lucy, Courtney Mallow, Leslie McDonald, Joe Medwid, Megan Mina, Patrick Nedley, Whitney Newton, Chris Oesterling, Farhad Omar, Cassandra Pagels, Melissa Pancurak, James Perakis, Graham Peterson, Zachary Pruckowski, Alison Quade, J. Quarles, Richard Rabbett, Rachel Robinson, Kevin Rouse, Tommy Schaperkotter, Shelley Schwartz, Heidi Shoemaker, Alison Singer, Adrian Sitler, Cole Smith, Ben Stephens, Katie Stranix, Malcolm Strickland, Francis Tan, Samantha Tognetti, Justin Urquhart, Clare van Montfrans, Juliana Villabona, Ryan Wall, Tessa Wheeler, Logan Whitehouse, Brian Williams, Michael Wilson, and Andrew Zacharias.

Chapter 7
Project 1800

The material for this case study was developed from interviews with Sally Harrison, architect and member of the faculty of Temple University; and Jon Musselman, construction manager with Habitat for Humanity Philadelphia (formerly Habitat for Humanity North Philadelphia.)

In addition to Sally Harrison, key members of the design team included Terry Jacobs, principal at Jacobs Wyper Architects; and John Collins, principal at The Delta Group and member of the faculty at Temple University; the Kachele Group, consulting engineers; RPA Associates, Inc., civil engineers; and Pahutski Land Surveying.

Chapter 8
Roxbury Estates

The material for this case study was developed from interviews with Rick Sundberg, former principal with Olson Sundberg Kundig Allen (now practicing as Rick Sundberg Architect); Dorothy Bullit, former executive director of Habitat for Humanity Seattle South King County; and Marty Kooistra, executive director of Habitat for Humanity Seattle South King County.

In addition to Rick Sundberg, key members of the Roxbury Estates design team included Stephen Yamada-Heidner, Brad Conway, Olivier Landa, Kristen Becker, Andrew Enright, Stephen Wood, Matthias Winkler, and Suzanne Zahr. Consultants for the project included Allworth Nessbaum

(landscape architect), Putnam Collins Scott (structural engineers), Keen Engineering and Greenbush Engineering (mechanical, electrical, and plumbing), Rosewater Engineering (civil). Callison Architecture prepared conceptual site planning and design for HFH Seattle South King County.

Chapter 9
Stiles Street Homes

The material for this case study was developed from interviews with Beth Miller and Linda Dotter of the Community Design Collaborative in Philadelphia; Maarten Pesch and Megan McGinley of Wallace, Roberts & Todd; Jon Musselman, construction manager for Habitat for Humanity Philadelphia; and Frank Monaghan, executive director of Habitat for Humanity Philadelphia.

In addition to Pesch and McGinley, other members of the Stiles Street project design team within WRT included Jean-Pierre Brokken, Harsha Desai, Maria Elosua, and Erin Monaghan. Consultants for the project included the Energy Coordinating Agency of Philadelphia, energy analysis and LEED provider; David Chou & Associates, structural engineer; Atkinson Koven Feinberg Engineers, mechanical engineering; and Pennoni Associates, Inc., geotechnical engineering.

Chapter 10
Stanley Street

The material for this case study was developed from interviews with Chuck Roberts, principal with Kuhn Riddle Architects, and M.J. Adams, executive director of Habitat for Humanity Pioneer Valley.

In addition to Roberts, key members of the project design team included James Brassord, director of Facilities, Amherst College; Tom Davies, assistant director of facilities/director of Design and Construction, Amherst College.

In addition to M.J. Adams, staff and volunteers from Habitat for Humanity Pioneer Valley involved in the project included Michael Broad, building construction superintendent, and Building Committee members: Steve Ferrari, Peter Jessop, Charlie Klem, and Walt Kohler.

Chapter 11
New Columbia Villa

The material for this case study was developed from interviews with Kim Pannan and Paul McKean, along with Steve Messinetti, executive director of Habitat for Humanity Portland/Metro East.

In addition to Pannan and McKean, key members of the project design team included Cornell Anderson, Noelle Elliot, Shem Harding, Monica Miller, Amy Running, and Edward Running.

Chapter 12
Webster Street

The material for this case study was developed from interviews with Scott Mooney, intern architect with Thomas Hacker Architects; David Posada, intern architect with GDB Architects; Dick Hutchinson with Walsh Construction; Carmen Schleiger, director of Housing Development with Habitat for Humanity Portland/Metro East; and Steve Messenetti, executive director for Habitat for Humanity Portland/Metro East.

In addition to Mooney and Posada, key members of the project design team included Howard Thurston, structural engineer; Kathy Bash, energy analysis, Jessica Green, landscape architect, Rebecca Novis, homes coordination; Randy Hansell, homes provider; and Dick Hutchison of Walsh Construction.

Chapter 13
Kinsell Commons at Tassafaronga Village
The material for this case study was developed from interviews with David Baker, principal, Daniel Simons, and Mark Hogan, David Baker and Partners Architects (DBPA); Natalie Monk, assistant project manager, Habitat for Humanity East Bay.
In addition to Baker, Simons, and Hogan, key members of the DBPA project design team included Mia Bhimani, Amanda Loper, Padma Mahadevan, Kevin Markarian, Sara Mae Martens, and Amit Price Patel. Consultants included Josiah Cain, landscape architect; Gener St. Onge, structural engineer, and Michael Kuykendall, civil engineer.

We would also like to acknowledge the support and encouragement provided by our colleagues at Auburn University. They provided the setting for our work with students and with Habitat, along with the space, support, and time to pursue this writing project.

No first-time authors can complete a book without lots of hand-holding from their publisher, and we are no exception. We are grateful to Routledge for this opportunity to share these projects with a larger audience. We are especially grateful for the support we have received from Wendy Fuller, Laura Williamson, Alfred Symons, and Alex Lazarou.

David Hinson and Justin Miller

REFERENCES

Preface

1   The Rural Studio is an outreach program of the School of Architecture, Planning, and Landscape Architecture at Auburn University. The program provides opportunities for architecture students to engage in community-based design/build projects targeted to serve low-income families and community organizations in the three-county region around the Rural Studio's Newbern, Alabama, campus. The Rural Studio was established in 1994 by Samuel Mockbee and D.K. Ruth. Since Mockbee's death in 2001, the Rural Studio has been led by Andrew Freear. Additional information regarding the Rural Studio, its projects, students, and clients can be found at www.ruralstudio.com.

2   Millard Fuller, interview with David Hinson, September 2001. David Hinson and sixteen Auburn architecture students visited Habitat for Humanity International's offices in Americus, Georgia, in September of 2001. Fuller hosted the group for lunch and offered these comments in the context of that meeting.

3   Bohl, Charles C. "Affordable Housing Design for Place Making and Community Building," Chapter 7 in *Chasing the American Dream: New Perspectives on Home Ownership*, edited by William M. Rohe and Harry L. Watson, p. 126, Ithaca and London: Cornell University Press, 2007.

4   Davis, Sam. *The Architecture of Affordable Housing*, p. 63, Berkeley: University of California Press, 1995.

5   Fuller, Millard. *A Simple, Decent Place to Live: The Building Realization of Habitat for Humanity*, pp. 13–27, Waco, Texas: Word Publishing (Habitat for Humanity), 1995.

6   Baggett, Jerome. *Habitat for Humanity: Building Private Homes, Building Public Religion*, p. 47, Philadelphia: Temple University Press, 2001.

7   "Myths (and facts) about Habitat for Humanity," www.hfhi.org.

8   Baggett, p. 176.

9   "Habitat for Humanity Fact Sheet," www.hfhi.org.

10 Baggett, p. 116.

11 Baggett, p. 168.

12 Baggett, p. 109.

13 Harrel, Evan. "Use of Design with Habitat for Humanity," Chapter 2 in *Good Deeds, Good Design: Community Service through Architecture*, edited by Bryan Bell, p. 74, New York: Princeton Architectural Press, 2004.

14 Baggett, p. 165, p. 169.

15 Duany, Andres, Plater-Zyberk, Elizabeth, and Speck, Jeff. *Suburban Nation: The Rise of Sprawl and the Decline of the American Dream*, p. 52, New York: North Point Press, 2000.

16 Habitat for Humanity International began to embrace energy conservation and sustainable construction practices in the late 1990s. Early initiatives included a "Green Team" of construction advisors from the HFHI headquarters staff who helped affiliates incorporate green design and construction practices and standards. HFHI has sustained this commitment to incorporating sustainable construction into its organizational culture. In 2008 HFHI launched the "Partners in Sustainable Building" program, underwritten by the Home Depot Foundation, which provides grants to affiliates and affiliate support organizations to integrate Energy Star certification into their building standards.

17 Davis, Sam. *The Architecture of Affordable Housing*, p. 11, Berkeley and Los Angeles: University of California Press, 1995.

18 Bohl, pp. 126–8.

19 Davis, p. 17.

20 Michael Pyatok, principal of Pyatok Architects Inc., has developed an extensive portfolio of award-winning affordable housing projects, accounting for over 35,000 units of housing in his four-decade career. More information on Pyatok's work can be found on the firm's website: www.pyatok.com.
    Pyatok has written about his approach to design in *Good Neighbors: Affordable Family Housing*, coauthored with Tom Jones and William Pettus, and published by Images Publishing Group in 1997.

21 Rohe, William M. and Watson, Harry L. "Introduction: Homeownership in American Culture and Public Policy," in *Chasing the American Dream: New Perspectives on Home Ownership*, edited by William M. Rohe and Harry L. Watson, p. 2, Ithaca and London: Cornell University Press, 2007.

22 Gutman, Robert. "Two Questions for Architecture," in *Good Deeds, Good Design: Community Service through Architecture*, edited by Bryan Bell, New York: Princeton Architectural Press, 2004.

23 "American Housing Survey for the United States: 2009 (H-150-07)." This document can be accessed online at www.census.gov.

24 The issue of limited data regarding the role of architects in the housing sector is covered in "Truth in Numbers, a Look at the Origin of Architecture's Motivational '2 percent' Statistic—and Why It's Wrong," authored by Suzanne LeBarre in *Metropolis Magazine*'s online blog "Metropolis Observed," October 15, 2008. www.metropolismag.com.

25 Baker, Kermit. *The 2006 AIA Firm Survey Report*, published by the American Institute of Architects. The 2006 AIA Firm Survey report reflects the involvement of professional architecture firms in the housing market prior to the collapse of the construction economy in 2008.

Chapter 1

1   More information about the DESIGNhabitat program at Auburn University can be found at the program's website: www.designhabitat.org.

2   The process and outcomes of the DESIGNhabitat 1 project are documented in "Shelter for the Soul: The DESIGNhabitat Report," authored by David Hinson. A pdf of this report is available on the DESIGNhabitat website: www.cadc.auburn.edu/design-habitat/resources.html.

3   The process and outcomes of the DESIGNhabitat 2 project are documented in "DESIGNhabitat 2: Studies in Prefab Affordable Housing," authored by David Hinson and Stacy Norman. A pdf of this report is available on the DESIGNhabitat website: www.cadc.auburn.edu/design-habitat/resources.html.

4   Hinson, David and Norman, Stacy. "DESIGNhabitat 2.0 & 2.1: Two Case Studies in Pre-Fab Affordable Housing," *Rebuilding, Proceedings of the 98th ACSA Annual Meeting*, edited by Bruce Goodwin and Judith Kinnard, p. 623, Washington, DC: ACSA Press, 2010.

Chapter 2

1   More information about the University of Arkansas Community Design Center can be found at the center's website: www.uacdc.uark.edu. The process and outcomes associated with the Habitat Trails project are documented in two publications: "Habitat Trails: A Manual for Affordable Green Neighborhood Development" and "Porches." Both documents are available on the above referenced website.

Chapter 3

1   Student comments regarding their experience of working on the VPH House can be found in online archives of articles about the project published in 2005. Examples include:
Vinyl by Design, "The Kind of Homework Architect Students Love," www.vinylindesign.com/HomePageContent/News/2005News/TheKindofHomeworkArchitectStudentsLove.aspx.
LSU Highlights, "LSU Architecture Students Design and Build Local Habitat for Humanity Home," www.lsu.edu/highlights/052/vinyl.html.

Chapter 4

1   More information about the "Partners in Sustainable Building" program can be found at www.habitat.org/newsroom/2008archive/03_21_08_Home_Depot.aspx?print=tr.

2   The process and outcomes of the DESIGNhabitat 3 studio can be found at www.designhabitat.org.

Chapter 5

1   More information about the habiTECH09 studio at Louisiana Tech University can be found at the program's website: www.habitech09.latech.edu.

Chapter 6

1   More information about the ecoMOD program at the University of Virginia can be found at the program's website: http://ecomod.virginia.edu/.

2   Information on the ecoMOD2 home is documented at: http://ecomod.virginia.edu/projects/prehab/.

3   Information on the ecoMOD4 home is documented at: http://ecomod.virginia.edu/projects/thru/.

Chapter 7

1   Harrison, Sally. "Inefficient by Design: Habitat for Humanity in North Philadelphia." A paper presented at the 2010 International Architectural Research Conference, June 24–26, 2010, Washington, DC. The conference was co-sponsored by the Architectural Research Centers Consortium and the European Association of Architectural Education. Published proceedings from the conference are pending.

Chapter 8

1   More information on the Roxbury Estates project can be found at www.olsonkundigarchitects.com/Projects/186/Habitat-for-Humanity-Roxbury-Estates.

Chapter 9

1   The Community Design Collaborative (CDC) is a volunteer-based non-profit community design center serving non-profit community organizations in the Philadelphia region. The CDC provides *pro-bono* preliminary design services via teams of professional volunteers drawn from the Philadelphia design and construction communities. More information about the CDC can be found at www.cdesignc.org.

2   The Energy Coordinating Agency (ECA) is a non-profit organization that provides services and support to "promote a sustainable and socially equitable energy future for all in the Philadelphia region." The ECA provided energy analysis assistance for the Stiles Street homes and served as the LEED provider on the project. More information on the ECA can be found at www.ecasavesenergy.org.

Chapter 10

1   More information about the Stanley Street project can be found on the Kuhn Riddle Architects website at http://kuhnriddle.com/portfolio/featured-sustainable/habitat-for-humanity/.
Additional information can also be found on the Habitat for Humanity Pioneer Valley website at www.pioneervalleyhabitat.org/newsletters/PVHnewsletterjune09.pdf.

Chapter 11

1   More information about the New Columbia Villa project can be found on the Paul McKean Architecture website at www.pmckean.com/community/habitat-for-humanity/.

Chapter 12

1   Details on the "Natural Talent Design Competition," sponsored by the US Green Building Council, can be found at the USGBC website: www.usgbc.org/DisplayPage.aspx?CMSPageID=257.

2   The green building strategies for the Webster Street homes are detailed on the Habitat for Humanity Portland/Metro East website. See: http://habitatportlandmetro.org/our-builds/green-building/.

3   Details regarding the Earth Advantage Homes program can be found at the Earth Advantage Institute website: www.earthadvantage.org.

Chapter 13

1   Details regarding the Tassafaronga Village project and the Kinsell Commons homes can be found at the Habitat for Humanity East Bay website: www.habitateb.org/kinsellcommons.

Lessons from the Field

1   Cary, John. "How to Pro Bono," in *The Power of Pro Bono*, edited by John Cary, p. 262, New York: Metropolis Books, 2010.

2   Abramowitz, Ava J. *Architect's Essentials of Negotiation*, 2nd Edition, Chapter 2, p. 18, Hoboken, New Jersey: John Wiley & Sons, Inc., 2009.

3   Peterson, John. "Why Pro Bono?" Preface to *The Power of Pro Bono*, edited by John Cary, p. xii, New York: Metropolis Books, 2010.

4   Blau, Judith. *Architects and Firms: A Sociological Perspective on Architectural Practice*, Cambridge: MIT Press, 1984.

5   Peterson. "Why Pro Bono?" p. xii.

6   Cary, John. "Architecture as a Social Act," in *The Power of Pro Bono*, edited by John Cary, p. 17, New York: Metropolis Books, 2010.

7   Davis, Sam. *The Architecture of Affordable Housing*, p. 63, Berkeley: University of California Press, 1995.

8   Baggett, Jerome. *Habitat for Humanity: Building Private Homes, Building Public Religion*, p. 65, Philadelphia: Temple University Press.

9   Abramowitz. p. 18.

RESOURCES

The resources listed below were compiled with the assistance of the thirteen project teams profiled in *Designed for Habitat*.

Books

25 Houses under 1500 Square Feet, by James Grayson Trulove. Published by Harper Design, 2005.

Affordable Housing: Designing an American Asset, by Adrianne Schmidtz. Published by the Urban Land Institute, 2005.

The Architecture of Affordable Housing, by Sam Davis. Published by the University of California Press, 1995.

Architectural Graphic Standards for Residential Construction, by Janet Rumbarger, Richard Vitullo, and Charles George Ramsey. Published by John Wiley & Sons, 2003.

Cradle to Cradle: Remaking the Way We Make Things, by William McDonough and Michael Braungart. Published by North Point Press, 2002.

A Decent Home: Planning, Building, and Preserving Affordable Housing, by Allan Mallach. Published by Planners Press (The American Planning Association), 2009.

Design for the Other 90 percent, by Cynthia E. Smith. Published by Editions Assouline, 2007.

Expanding Architecture: Design as Activism, edited by Bryan Bell and Katie Wakeford. Published by Metropolis Books, 2008.

Good Neighbors: Affordable Family Housing, by Tom Jones, William Pettis, and Michael Pyatok. Published by McGraw-Hill, 1997.

Graphic Guide to Frame Construction, by Rob Thallon. Published by Taunton Press, 2008.

The Green House: New Directions in Sustainable Architecture, by Alanna Stang and Christopher Hawthorne. Published by the Princeton Architectural Press, 2010.

The Green Studio Handbook (2nd Edition), by Alison G. Kwok and Walter T. Grondzik. Published by Architectural Press, 2011.

Habitat for Humanity: How to Build a House, by Larry Haun. Published by Taunton Press, 2002.

The Home House Project: The Future of Affordable Housing, edited by David Brown. Published by MIT Press, 2005.

Homes within Reach: A Guide to the Planning, Design, and Construction of Affordable Homes and Communities, by Avi Friedman. Published by John Wiley & Sons, 2005.

Housing as if People Mattered, by Clare Cooper Marcus and Wendy Sarkissian. Published by University of California Press, 1988.

Low Impact Development: A Design Manual for Urban Areas, by the University of Arkansas Community Design Center. Published by University of Arkansas Press, 2010. This book is available from the UACDC website: http://uacdc.uark.edu, as well as online bookstores and national design and planning conventions.

A Pattern Book for Neighborly Houses: Details and Techniques for Building and Renovating Neighborly Houses, by the US area office of Habitat for Humanity International and the Institute of Classical Architecture and Classical America, 2007.

The Perfect $100,000 House: A Trip Across America and Back in Pursuit of a Place to Call Home, by Karrie Jacobs. Published by Viking Press, 2006.

The Prefabricated Home, by Colin Davies. Published by Reaktion Books, 2005.

PreFab Green, by Michelle Kaufmann and Kathy Remick. Published by Gibbs Smith, 2006.

Prefab Modern, by Jill Herbers. Published by Harper Design, 2006.

Refabricating Architecture, by Stephen Kieran and James Timberlake. Published by McGraw-Hill, 2003.

Rural Studio: Samuel Mockbee and an Architecture of Decency, by Andrea Oppenheimer Dean and Timothy Hursley. Published by Princeton Architectural Press, 2002.

Sustainable, Affordable, Prefab: The ecoMOD Project, by John D. Quale. Published by University of Virginia Press, 2011.

Web-based Resources

Habitat for Humanity Construction Technologies

"Habitat for Humanity's US and international affiliates build durable, healthy, and sustainable houses at the lowest possible cost. This website provides information and training resources for sustainable building, energy efficiency, safe and healthy housing, and construction."

>> www.habitat.org/env/default.aspx

BuildingGreen.com

Building Green is "an independent company committed to providing accurate, unbiased, and timely information designed to help building-industry professionals and policy makers improve the environmental performance, and reduce the adverse impacts, of buildings."

>> www.buildinggreen.com/

Building Science Corporation

"Building Science Corporation provides objective, high-quality information about commercial and residential buildings. This resource combines building physics, systems design concepts, and an awareness of sustainability to promote the design and construction of buildings that are more durable, healthier, more sustainable and more economical than most buildings built today."

>> www.buildingscience.com

The Affordable Housing Design Advisor

Design Advisor is a collection of best-practice design guidelines and case study examples developed by the US Department of Housing and Urban Development.

>> www.designadvisor.org/

National Fenestration Rating Council

NFRC develops and administers energy-related rating and certification programs that serve the public by providing fair, accurate, and credible information on fenestration performance.

>> www.nfrc.org/

US Department of Housing and Urban Development (HUD)

HUD's mission is to create strong, sustainable, inclusive communities and quality affordable homes for all. HUD is working to strengthen the housing market to bolster the economy and protect consumers; meet the need for quality affordable rental homes; utilize housing as a platform for improving quality of life; build inclusive and sustainable communities free from discrimination; and transform the way HUD does business. HUD provides advice on buying a home, renting, default, foreclosure avoidance, credit issues and reverse mortgages.

>> http://portal.hud.gov/hudportal/HUD?src=/i_want_to/talk_to_a_housing_counselor

US Green Building Council (USGBC)

The USGBC is a "non-profit community of leaders working to make green buildings available to everyone within a generation." The USGBC developed the Leadership in Energy and Environmental Design (LEED) building certification and verification system.

>> www.usgbc.org/

Florida Solar Energy Center (FSEC)

The FSEC has partnered with more than fifty Habitat for Humanity affiliates through the Building America Partners program (US Department of Energy). "The partnership has generated a rich body of collective experience from 'blitz' builds, as well as a cohesive set of web based and hardcopy documents that give HFH affiliates practical guidance on energy efficiency, indoor air quality, combustion safety, moisture mitigation, and 'green' building." Information on FSEC's work with Habitat for Humanity is available on its website.

>> www.fsec.ucf.edu/en/media/newsletters/echron/archives/2006/Q4/baihp-habitat_for_humanity.htm

The Building America program

"Sponsored by the US Department of Energy (DOE), the Building America program ... acts as a national residential test bed where different building system options are evaluated, designed, built, retrofitted, and vetted to ensure that requirements for energy efficiency, quality, sustainability, risk mitigation, and comfort are met. Research is conducted on individual measures and systems, test houses, and community-scale housing in order to validate the reliability, cost-effectiveness, and marketability of technologies when integrated into existing and new homes."

>> www1.eere.energy.gov/buildings/building_america/

For more information on Building America Partnership with Habitat for Humanity, see:

>> http://www.baihp.org/casestud/hfh_partner/index.htm

Green Building Advisor

A product of Taunton Press, publisher of *Fine Homebuilding*, GreenBuildingAdvisor.com draws on more than twenty-five years of experience publishing residential construction information; and is dedicated to providing the most useful, accurate, and complete information about designing, building, and remodeling energy-efficient, sustainable, and healthy homes.

>> www.greenbuildingadvisor.com/

Green Home Guide

Provided by USGBC, the website is a resource for green home expertise, ideas and connections, articles, insights and tips from experienced green professionals.

>> http://greenhomeguide.com/

Mother Earth News

"The most popular and longest running sustainable-lifestyle magazine, Mother Earth News provides wide-ranging, expert editorial coverage of organic foods, country living, green transportation, renewable energy, natural health and green building. Lively, insightful and on the cutting edge, Mother Earth News is the definitive read for the growing number of Americans who choose wisely and live well."

>> www.motherearthnews.com/home.aspx

ToolBase

"NAHB Research Center's ToolBase.org is the housing industry's best resource for technical information on building products, materials, new technologies, business management, and housing systems. The NAHB Research Center is a full-service product commercialization company that strives to make housing more durable and affordable by helping to push new building technologies into the residential market through our integrated consulting services. With nearly fifty years of accumulated residential construction and market expertise, the Research Center provides clients with an unrivaled depth of understanding of the housing industry and access to its business leaders."

>> www.toolbase.org/index.aspx

Energy Efficiency and Renewable Energy (EERE) Homes

The US Department of Energy funds research to develop energy-efficient and renewable energy technologies, practices, and products for homes.

>> www.energysavers.gov/
>> www.eere.energy.gov/topics/homes.html
>> www1.eere.energy.gov/buildings/residential_landing.html

AIA 50 to 50

"The AIA's 50 to 50 is a set of 50 strategies toward 50 percent fossil fuel reduction in buildings and provides a 'how-to' resource for architects and the construction industry. The 50 strategies represent readily available and effective tools and techniques that will have an immediate impact on architects' ability to achieve significant carbon reduction. They span a spectrum from broad-based site and planning objectives to specific, building-based concepts. Each strategy includes an overview of the subject, typical applications, emerging trends, links to information sources, and important relationships to other carbon reduction strategies."

>> www.aia.org/practicing/groups/kc/AIAS077430
>> http://wiki.aia.org/Wiki percent20Pages/Home.aspx

Sustainable Design and Construction Certification Program Links

Passivehaus Certification
>> www.passivehouse.us/passiveHouse/PHIUSHome.html

Leadership in Energy and Environmental Design (LEED)
>> www.usgbc.org/DisplayPage.aspx?CategoryID=19

Energy Star Homes (US Environmental Protection Agency)
>> www.energystar.gov/

Earth Advantage New Homes (Earth Advantage Institute)
>> www.earthadvantage.org

Green Point Rated Homes (Build It Green)
>> www.builditgreen.org/about/

Design and Energy Analysis Software Tools

RES*check*™

"The RES*check* materials have been developed to simplify and clarify code compliance with the Model Energy Code (MEC), the International Energy Conservation Code (IECC), and a number of state codes. The RES*check* residential compliance materials offer two ways to demonstrate compliance: the trade-off approach and the prescriptive packages approach."

>> www.energycodes.gov/rescheck/

HEED: Home Energy Efficient Design

"This user-friendly energy design tool shows how much money you can save by making changes to your home. It also shows how much greenhouse gas (including CO2) it accounts for, and its annual total energy consumption. HEED (Home Energy Efficient Design) works equally well for remodeling projects or designing new buildings."

>> www.aud.ucla.edu/energy-design-tools

Climate Consultant 5

"Free, easy-to-use, graphic-based computer program that displays climate data in dozens of ways useful to architects, builders, contractors, and homeowners, including temperatures, humidity, wind velocity, sky cover, and solar radiation in both 2-D and 3-D graphics for every hour of the year in either Metric or Imperial units. ... Climate Consultant 3.0 reads climate data in the EPW format that the Department of Energy makes available at no cost (in fact there are more than 1300 stations from around the world available in this format)."

>> www.aud.ucla.edu/energy-design-tools

EnergyPlus

"Next generation building energy simulation program that builds on the most popular features and capabilities of BLAST and DOE-2. EnergyPlus includes innovative simulation capabilities including time steps of less than an hour, modular systems simulation modules that are integrated with a heat balance-based zone simulation and input and output data structures tailored to facilitate third party interface development. Recent additions include multi-zone airflow, electric power simulation including fuel cells and other distributed energy systems, and water manager that controls and reports water use throughout the building systems, rainfall, groundwater, and zone water use."

>> www.energyplus.gov

Google Sketchup

Google's Sketchup is a free, open 3-D modeling software that has the ability to perform energy simulations using the Department of Energy's Open Studio (an EnergyPlus plugin created for Sketchup).

>> http://sketchup.google.com/
>> http://apps1.eere.energy.gov/buildings/energyplus/openstudio.cfm

Building Energy Software Tools Directory

"This directory provides information on 395 building software tools for evaluating energy efficiency, renewable energy, and sustainability in buildings. The energy tools listed in this directory include databases, spreadsheets, component and systems analyses, and whole-building energy performance simulation programs. A short description is provided for each tool along with other information including expertise required, users, audience, input, output, computer platforms, programming language, strengths, weaknesses, technical contact, and availability."

>> http://apps1.eere.energy.gov/buildings/tools_directory/

GLOSSARY

Alabama Energykey is a green building rating system sponsored by the Alabama Home Builders Association. More information can be found at: www.energykeyhome.com/index.html.

Bioswale refers to a topographic landscape feature used to temporarily collect and filter surface stormwater. More information can be found at: www.asla.org/guidesandtoolkit.aspx.

Charrette is a term that describes an intense design activity. The term is thought to have emerged in the nineteenth century at the École des Beaux-Arts in Paris. The term describes the intense design activity of architecture students that occurred shortly before and lasted until a project deadline. Today the term is used to describe a workshop in which key stakeholders work together to generate and discuss design ideas early in the design phase of a project.

Computer Numerically Controlled (CNC) equipment refers to tools, such as routers, that are given a set of instructions (often from drawings produced in 3-D modeling software) directing the path of the tool through space in order to cut, shape, or form materials with a high degree of precision.

EarthCraft-Certified Homes is a regional green building rating system developed in 1999 by the South Face Energy Institute and the Greater Atlanta Home Builders Association. EarthCraft homes can be found throughout the Southeast in the United States. More information can be found at: www.earthcraft.org.

Energy Star Certified Homes are houses designed to exceed the energy conservation standards of the 2004 International Residential Code (IRC) by at least 15 percent. To achieve Energy Star certification a builder must work with a certified, third-party energy rater to verify features and performance of the completed house. More information can be found at: www.energystar.gov.

Fiber-Cement Siding (Panels) is an alternative siding to wood or vinyl siding. "Fiber-cement siding is composed of cement, sand, and cellulose fiber that has been autoclaved (cured with pressurized steam) to increase its strength and dimensional stability. The fiber is added as reinforcement to prevent cracking. The planks come in 5¼" to 12" widths and 5/16" and 7/16" thickness." The siding is termite resistant, water resistant and non-combustible; manufacturers' warranties are often fifty years. More information can be found at: www.toolbase.org/Techinventory/TechDetails.aspx?ContentDetailID=4006&BucketID=2&CategoryID=42.

FSC-Certified Wood is a term describing wood products that have met the standards of the Forest Stewardship Council's (FSC) "responsible" harvesting criteria. FSC forest products are "verified from the forest of origin through the supply chain." More information can be found at: www.fsc.org/.

Green Point Rated Homes refers to homes designed and constructed to the standards developed by Build It Green, "a membership supported non-profit organization whose mission is to promote healthy, energy- and resource-efficient homes in California." More information can be found at: www.builditgreen.org/greenpoint percent2Drated.

Home Energy Rating System (HERS) Index refers to a scoring system in which a home built to meet the 2006 International Energy Conservation Code scores a HERS Index of 100. The lower the score the better, e.g. a HERS Index of 70 represents a 30 percent energy savings over code compliance and a "net zero energy" home is scored a HERS Index of 0. The system was established by the Residential Energy Services Network (RESNET). More information can be found at: www.resnet.us/home-energy-ratings.

HUD-Code Homes are factory-constructed, manufactured systems-built homes built in accordance with HUD (US Department of Housing and Urban Development) Code. Often referred to as mobile homes, HUD Code-homes unlike homes constructed on a permanent site are required to be built on a chassis. Details regarding the HUD Code can be found at: www.access.gpo.gov/nara/cfr/waisidx_01/24cfr3280_01.html.

Insulated Concrete Formwork (ICF) refers to lightweight, rigid plastic foam forms that hold concrete in place during curing and remain in place afterwards to serve as thermal insulation for concrete walls. More information can be found at: www.toolbase.org/Techinventory/TechDetails.aspx?ContentDetailID=602&BucketID=6&CategoryID=54.

LEED® for Homes is a national green building rating system developed by the US Green Building Council (USGBC). More information can be found at: www.usgbc.org.

Light Tubes are small, often tubular skylights that are utilized to bring daylight into interior rooms or where additional daylight is needed. Due to their size, light tubes suffer significantly lower heat loss and gain compared with a conventional skylight. More information can be found at: www.toolbase.org/Techinventory/TechDetails.aspx?ContentDetailID=4061&BucketID=2&CategoryID=42.

Low-Impact Development (LID) refers to the practice of minimizing environmental impact of development through a series of best-practice measures and techniques. LIDs balance the need for growth and environmental protection by focusing on minimizing land disturbance, increasing site density while maintaining open space for protection of local land and water resources. More information can be found at: www.asla.org/guidesandtoolkit.aspx.

Marmoleum Flooring is a type of linoleum flooring that is made of primarily natural raw materials. Comprised of linseed oil, rosins, and wood flour on a jute backing, the material is a very durable floor covering. More information can be found at: www.greenerbuilding.org/index.php.

Modular Construction refers to the use of factory-built modules or portions of homes. Also a form of systems-built homes, they are engineered and fabricated in a factory and shipped to the construction site to be set on a permanent foundation system.

Net Zero Energy Use (also net zero energy consumption) is a term used to describe a building in which there is zero net energy consumption and zero carbon emissions annually.

Optimum Value Engineered (OVE) Framing, also referred to as "advanced framing," is a method of framing that minimizes the amount of wood used to frame a building. The framing technique requires additional bracing, but uses fewer framing members at openings and corners, reducing thermal bridging common in conventional framing. More information can be found at: www.toolbase.org/Techinventory/Tech-Details.aspx?ContentDetailID=625&BucketID=6&CategoryID=13.

Panelized Construction refers to the use of prefabricated, or "factory built," panels to form the structural envelope of a building. Panelized wall systems may utilize a range of material assemblies including sheathed 2 × 4 (or 6) wood framing, light gauge steel framing, and SIPs. More information can be found at: www.toolbase.org/PDF/DesignGuides/PanelizedWallSystems_TechSpec.pdf.

Pervious Concrete Paving refers to concrete paving systems designed to allow stormwater to pass through voids in the material and seep into the ground rather than run off the surface of the paving. More information can be found at www.perviouspavement.org/.

Photovoltaic (PV) Panels are part of a solar electric system. Photovoltaic panels directly convert the sun's energy into electricity. This conversion requires no moving parts, is silent, and pollution free in its operation. The solar electricity is converted to utility-grade electricity, through balance of system components, for use directly in the home.

Polygal™ is a double-wall translucent plastic panel, often used in greenhouses and atria. More information can be found at: www.polygalnorthamerica.com/index.php.

Radiant Heating Systems supply heat directly to the floor or to panels in the wall or ceiling of a house. The systems depend largely on radiant heat transfer: the delivery of heat directly from the hot surface to the people and objects in the room via the radiation of heat, which is also called infrared radiation. See www.energysavers.gov/your_home/space_heating_cooling/index.cfm/mytopic=12590.

Rain Barrels are vessels connected to a gutter or downspout system to collect rainwater from roofs, and are often utilized for site irrigation. More information can be found at: www.toolbase.org/Techinventory/TechDetails.aspx?ContentDetailID=918&BucketID=6&CategoryID=11.

Rain Screen Cladding is a method for deterring rainwater intrusion into wall assemblies by providing separation between the rain barrier of a building and the exterior cladding. Rain screen cladding can be made of most conventional cladding materials. Rain screens shed most of the rain that impacts the cladding and manage the rest through the use of a drainage plane. See: www.toolbase.org/Techinventory/TechDetails.aspx?ContentDetailID=1020&BucketID=6&CategoryID=54.

REM/RATE is a residential energy analysis, code compliance and rating software developed by the Architectural Energy Corporation specifically for the needs of HERS providers. More information can be found at: www.archenergy.com/products/remrate.

Smart Meters are (electric) meters that provide "real-time" feedback on energy use, compared with traditional electrical meters, which measure the total consumption of electricity in a home over a day. More information can be found at: www.smartgrid.gov/the_smart_grid#smart_home.

Stormwater Gardens (also called rain gardens) are shallow, bowl-shaped landforms, planted with native perennial plants, designed to create a ponding area reducing the amount of stormwater entering stormwater systems or nearby bodies of water. More information can be found at: www.asla.org/guidesandtoolkit.aspx.

Structural Insulated Panel System (SIPS) is a form of panelized wall system consisting of a layer of foam insulation (polystyrene or polyurethane) sandwiched between two layers of oriented strand board (OSB), plywood, or fiber cement. SIPs are used for wall, roof, and floor framing, and have excellent insulation values. The panels are manufactured and delivered to site where they are assembled on site-built foundations. More information can be found at: www.toolbase.org/PDF/DesignGuides/SIPs_TechSpec.pdf.

Super-Insulated Houses refers to an approach to home construction that dramatically reduces heat loss (and gain) by using much higher levels of insulation and airtightness than normal. There is no set definition of super-insulation, but super-insulated buildings typically include very high levels of insulation along with details to ensure insulation continuity where walls meet roofs, foundations, and other walls. Super-insulated homes also emphasize airtight construction, especially around doors and windows. As a consequence of the emphasis on insulation values, super-insulated homes require much smaller than conventional heating and air-conditioning systems.

Sweat Equity refers to the 500 hours of their own labor that Habitat for Humanity partner families invest in building their own house and in the construction of homes for other partner families. Habitat for Humanity affiliates partition these hours in accordance with the specific circumstances of location. More information can be found at: www.habitat.org/how/factsheet.aspx.

Switched Electric Receptacles refer to a simple way to control the electrical loads associated with appliances, televisions, and other devices that draw electricity to power clocks and other built-in devices even when not in use. Connecting receptacles to wall switches allows these devices to be turned off and helps home owners conserve electricity from these so-called "phantom" loads.

Wood-Fiber Cement Block (Faswall®) refers to a form of stay-in-place insulated concrete forms (ICFs) constructed of cement-bonded recycled wood chips. The blocks are lightweight and are available with mineral fiber insulation to provide an energy-efficient, fire- and termite-resistant, and durable structural wall system. More information can be found at: www.toolbase.org/Techinventory/TechDetails.aspx?ContentDetailID=614&BucketID=6&CategoryID=54.

CREDITS

The authors wish to thank the many generous contributors to this publication. Their work helps make the stories of these projects come alive.

INDEX